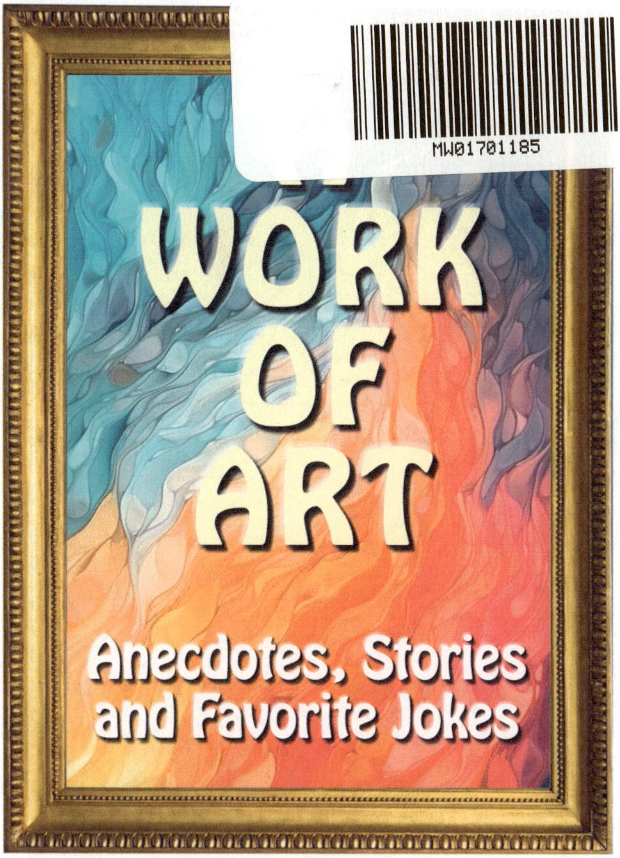
WORK
OF
ART
Anecdotes, Stories
and Favorite Jokes

A WORK OF ART

Anecdotes, Stories and Favorite Jokes

Art Albritton

Another Quality Book Published By:

LEGACY Book Publishing

1850 Lee Rd., STE. 223 Winter Park, FL 32789

www.LEGACYBOOKPUBLISHING.com

A Work of Art
Anecdotes, Stories, and Favorite Jokes

Published by:
LEGACY Book Publishing
1850 Lee Road, Suite 223
Winter Park, Florida 32789
www.LegacyBookPublishing.com

Printed in the United States
ISBN: 978-1-958923-45-0

Cover Design by Gabriel H. Vaughn
Edited by Melina Redondo

Preface

Recently, I began writing down a few anecdotes that have occurred in my wonderful life. The number of them began to grow, and since many of them were about my extended family, I thought that maybe I should write a book. Well, the anecdotes kept growing in number and included a range of events from my life: from working at State Farm Insurance Companies, to fishing trips, and more.

I also had some fun experiences sharing jokes with others, which made me realize that I wanted to share my favorite jokes in this book too. Many of them have become so well known to my wife, Nita, that we can share just one line from the story and experience great laughter.

It has been a wonderful experience to put this book together. I hope that reading it will be a wonderfully entertaining experience for you. I sincerely hope that your life can be as much fun as mine has been.

EAA

Anecdotes and Stories Introduction

These anecdotes and stories, some short and some long, relate primarily to the joys in my life. Some of them are lessons learned along the way, and some of them are just the fun times experienced. After writing and reviewing them all, I can't help but better understand what a wonderful time life is!

Anecdotes and Stories Index

Lake Fun!

Living on Lake Idylwild, the children always had fun on the water. Christi was an avid water skier. For Christmas, she really wanted a slalom ski. She could already ride on one ski rather than two but wanted to be able to do all the fancy cutting back and forth. Santa brought her the ski and as luck would have it, Florida weather on Christmas was pretty cold! She was determined to ride it on Christmas morning, and so we did! After pulling her with the boat for a trip around the lake, I was cold, so we stopped. She was turning blue but was still excited about her new Christmas ski.

Alex and Andrew, born 22 years after Christi, loved tubing and wakeboarding. Tubing was less challenging

Riding the tubes with friends.

but more fun because they could ride along with their friends all at the same time. Guest friends included Randy, Travis, Robbie, Trevor, Ben, Tyler, Austin, Brad, Stephen, Charlie, Chase, Drew, Tre, and Cody. I bought two tubes to pull behind the boat and tied the ropes at the exact same length for safety reasons. When they would swing and bang the tubes together, it was like bumper cars on water. Their goal was to knock the other one off the tube and into the lake water. It was fun for them beyond description.

They then decided that it would be fun to stand up on the tube rather than lying down on it. This took some practice—not to mention balance—since the tube was not only moving, but flexible too. They soon mastered this and were ready to create another challenge. Now they decided that it would be fun to try to jump from one tube to the other tube, so that they would both be on the same tube. They became quite proficient at doing so. When they had friends over, I would pull a guest boy on one tube and Alex or Andrew on the second tube. When the tubes came close, Alex or Andrew would jump on the other kid's tube much to his surprise. Sometimes they immediately fell off and sometimes, if the empty tube came close, they jumped back on their own tube. Finally, some of their friends learned to jump tubes, and while pulling two boys on each tube, all four of them ended up on the same tube. Some were lying down, some standing up, and all having a great time even after crashing into the water.

Wakeboarding was more of an individual sport. It took more strength, stamina, and balance just to get up on top of the water. Then the tricks of riding backward, sideways, turning flips, and other challenges came. Alex and Andrew became quite proficient at them all, as did a few of their friends, but the wakeboard required more delays in getting a turn—which is why tubing was more fun with a lot of friends over.

Great, great fun on the lake for all my children and their friends!

Alex and Andrew tubing with my grandkids, Ellie and Daniel.

Art Near Drowning

When I was very young, my family visited relatives who had rented the Feinberg cottage right on Crooked Lake. A number of children were in the water swimming and having fun. I was one of them, and although I couldn't swim, I was floating around on an inflated inner tube. My Uncle Edwin was sitting on the dock watching us have fun in the lake. One of the older kids swimming underwater came up for air and accidentally knocked me off the tube. My memory of the event is that since I couldn't swim, I just went down and sat on the bottom of the lake. Almost immediately, my uncle was pulling me up. I can assure you of this, I learned to swim after that!

First Childbirth

When the first real contractions began, we headed to the hospital. After we had been there for a while, the contractions stopped! I had planned to stay at the hospital all night until the event was over, and Christi was born. The nurse came in and insisted that I go home and get some rest. Insisted, insisted, insisted! She would call me if the contractions started again. Finally, I agreed and left.

Christi's mom was "certain" that I was out in the lobby and convinced the nursing staff to roll her bed out there so she could see me.

Obviously, she didn't see me! Early the next morning I returned to the hospital, contractions began again, and a healthy daughter Christi was born.

Teacher Confrontation

While Christi was in elementary school, one of her teachers was talking to another teacher about Christi and said, "She doesn't have sense enough to come in out of the rain." The conversation between the two teachers was overheard by Heidi, a friend of Christi. Heidi repeated the story to Christi who then repeated the story to me. Obviously, something needed to be done.

The next morning, I was at the school with an appointment to see the teacher during her free period. She had no idea why I was there since Christi was an outstanding student. She opened the meeting with, "I'm surprised to see you. Why are you here?"

I said, "I am here because you said that Christi doesn't have sense enough to come in out of the rain!"

She immediately was flustered, embarrassed, and extremely apologetic. She wanted to call Christi right then and apologize to her, but I wanted more conversation and details. When we finished our conversation, she called Christi in and apologized while I was there.

I'm pretty sure that she never made the mistake of criticizing a student in public again. I felt pretty good defending my daughter and any other students that she might say negative things about.

Mother's Cooking

My mother's cooking can best be described as typical southern-style cooking. She always served one or two meats, an unusually large number of side dishes, and plenty of desserts.

It always amazed me how she could take dishes with regular names and transform them into her specialties when she cooked them. I will try to list a few: warm potato salad, mac & cheese, ham and ham rice, roast beef and gravy, homemade biscuits (made with lard), and of course, lemon or butterscotch meringue pies. Sweet tea was a must!

She was so amazing at making all of the chosen dishes for dinner in the small kitchen that measured 11x7 not counting the kitchen cabinets. Working space was sufficient for two people if no one else came through. I can tell you that the food was sensational. But I can also tell you that when the cooking was over, the tiny kitchen was overflowing with pots and pans. On Sundays, all the kids did the dishes since we did not work in the orange groves that day. What a job the cleanup was!

On Saturdays, one of my jobs was to disc the orange groves. One of the groves was in Alturas, Florida. It took about 45 minutes each way to drive the tractor and tow the disc to the grove, and the job wasn't finished until well after lunch. My mother would bring a hot lunch with a half-gallon of her sweet tea! What a sight to see her coming down the road for her tired, hot, hungry, thirsty working son! Moms are the best!

After our Sunday noon meals, everyone would stay at the table, lean back on the back two legs of the dining room chair, place a knee on the edge of the table, and have family conversations. Everything was discussed and everyone's thoughts were welcome. I am so thankful that I grew up in a family with open communication that valued the opinions of everyone. When conversations were finished, it was time for the kids to clean up the kitchen dishes! Maybe that was the real reason that everyone participated in the conversations!!

Steak Eating Pressure

While visiting relatives in Miami (without my dad), we had a steak dinner. I got full from all the great food and didn't wish to finish eating my steak. Many of my relatives began pressuring me to finish my food because of the expense of the steaks.

When we returned home, I was still upset about it and told my dad. He said, "I would have laid a $20 bill on the table and said, 'that should cover it!'"

No one, not even my dad, ever knew how much his response changed my life in feeling good, worthy, useful, and important as a person.

The Greatest Gift

Just before Christmas 2023, I had an inspiration for a Christmas gift for Nita, but there was not enough time to get it before Christmas. It was still a wonderful idea for a gift.

The inspiration came from a recording of "Frontier Christmas" that I heard from an LP vinyl record of Nita's parents, Max and Billie Day. The record was recorded by two comedy guys named Hudson & Landry. For the upcoming 2023 Christmas, we found the story on CD and ordered it for our listening enjoyment. Words cannot compete with listening to it, but I'll try to describe the basics of the story.

It was Christmas and the pioneer woman was remembering the music box that her husband had bought her. They had to sell it on the way out west for supplies and groceries. The man's sidekick Indian was away on a secret mission to try to find it and buy it. He returns with the gift and the man gives it to his wife. When she opens the gift, she says, "It's my music box." They kiss and it is a wonderful, emotional ending. And so, the first part of my inspiration for a gift was born.

Every Christmas Eve, late at night after all of the Christmas things are finished, Nita and I listen, sing, and dance to the song "The Greatest Gift of All" by Kenny Rogers and Dolly Parton. Our favorite line from the song is "knowing you're in love with me, is the greatest gift of all." This song and its words were the second part of my inspiration for the gift.

The next part of the plan was to purchase a music box, but only if it was possible to have that portion of the song played when the music box was opened.

The final part was that this must be a total surprise to Nita! Since she reviews all our credit card

"It's My Music Box."

statements as well as all our bank statements, secrecy is a huge problem! It seems like there are too many obstacles for my creative inspiration for the perfect gift. I finally got an idea to solve this problem as well as a few others.

My sister-in-law, Debbie Smith, who lives in Auburn, Alabama could pay for it on her credit card and the surprise factor would work! Also, I needed her help in picking out a music box that is beautiful enough to be loved and cherished by Nita. Debbie was a wonderful help through it all.

After contacting Music Box Attic in California, they assured me that the desired music was available, the engraving would be done as I desired, and a few other things that I wanted would be added. Debbie helped me choose the perfect music box, and the order was placed with the gift to be sent to her Alabama address.

A trip was already planned for us to visit Debbie, and we were hoping that the gift would be delivered while we were there. It arrived, and Debbie wrapped it beautifully without Nita knowing anything. Nita was totally surprised when I handed her a gift. She opened it and seeing the gift said, "It's my music box." She then opened the lid, and it played the song, "knowing you're in love with me, is the greatest gift of all."

Through many tears of joy, we danced, hugged, and cried and it all was wonderful. The present wasn't the greatest gift of all, but it says it all, and will be a cherished gift forever!

Teflon Nickname

While our kids were playing baseball, I became good friends with Danny Gill, a local funeral director. I will be friends with anyone—you never know when you will need them.

Danny decided that my nickname was "Teflon." I asked him why and he said, "Because nothing sticks to you. You can say anything, and it just rolls off people. You get away with saying anything, even with Nita!"

I have also heard similar comments at work. Coworkers were always telling me that they couldn't believe the things that I could get away with saying in management meetings.

Life's a slippery slope. I think I can live with the occasional "Teflon" comments.

T-Ball

Baseball was always Andrew's first love in sports. Alex was much less enthusiastic in the early years, though he did become great at it later. Andrew's enthusiasm started even before T-ball. At the age of four, I would pitch the ball to him, and he could hit it with a bat. If no baseball equipment was around, he would wad up something he found, make it into a ball, pick up a stick, and say, "pitch it to me" —and he could hit it!

We were at the local Little League field, and I was pitching to him when he was four and a local newspaper photographer came by. Andrew was hitting the ball and the photographer wanted to take a picture. The picture appeared in the local paper!

The first year both Alex and Andrew played T-ball, they were four-and-a-half years old and were allowed to play if Nita was dugout mom. The second year, Alex decided not to play. The first year, it was obvious how much Andrew loved the game and the effort he put forth. The second year, he was really good for only being 5 years old. The coach told me, "He amazes me every game with the things he does and how hard he tries." Andrew was selected to play the position of pitcher, which was one of the hardest positions in T-ball. In T-ball, the kids don't pitch, but every ball is thrown to the pitcher to stop play. Most kids at the age of 5 cannot catch the ball so the runners just keep running. Andrew could catch the ball almost every time! Andrew was also a good hitter but was looking forward to hitting a home run like one of the bigger kids had done.

The next year, Andrew was 6 years old, and all his efforts paid off for him and he became a star player. All the kids wanted to be "like Andrew," though one or two were jealous because he could catch everything. He also hit an "inside the park" home run which made him very happy. Andrew was almost the only player that could field a hit ball and throw the runner out. He also was the only player on the team that could catch a fly ball. That always got an ovation from the crowd since so few could do it at that age.

It was a great two years for Andrew in T-ball. Later, he would have to share the limelight with Alex, but for now he was the shining star and loved the chance to play baseball!

Future allstar

NEWS CHIEF 2-9-98

ANDREW ALBRITTON, 4 1/2, shows some real concentration on the pitch that his father, Art Albritton, tosses his way. The two were hard at work Sunday afternoon at Sertoma Park. — *Jonathan Dyer/News Chief*

Hitting pitches before T-ball. (February 9, 1998)

Pitch? No!!

In Little League Baseball, Alex played 3rd base and had never pitched. Also, he had never practiced pitching. He was, however, one of the bigger kids. Most kids consider pitching to be their dream job in Little League Baseball. The pitcher was struggling, and the coach came to the mound and said "Alex, you're now pitching." Alex said to the coach, "I'm not pitching." And he didn't! Later, after practicing how to pitch, he did pitch and became quite a success at it.

He still is a strong-willed person and responds similarly if he is told what to do! (I am told that he gets this from his father)!

Championship Pitching

Alex was pitching in the region's JV championship game for local high schools. We were leading, but Alex was struggling some as our pitcher. The coach was trying to determine whether to replace him, but decided to leave him in, telling him that he was on a "short leash." Alex continued pitching with relievers ready and pitched the whole game. We won the championship and after the team piled on top of him in celebration, the team trophy was handed to Alex for his outstanding pitching performance, and for being MVP of the game. The determination demonstrated in that game still gives him confidence when handling difficult challenges today.

Never Strike Out

When Andrew was 12 years old and playing baseball, his goal was to never strike out. As the season went along, the parents in the crowd as well as the team, began to notice and say, “Andrew never strikes out.” And so, it continued for many games.

He played the whole season and never truly struck out, with the only exception being that he made contact and it fouled off the bat, but as luck would have it, it went right into the catcher’s mitt for an out!

During that same year, he was called in as a relief pitcher for his brother, Alex. Alex was our ace pitcher but at the beginning of one inning, he was struggling a little and the coach decided to make a change and brought in Andrew to pitch. Andrew struck out the next three batters much to the excitement of Alex, the team, and the spectators!

Coach’s Job

My son Andrew was playing baseball at the age of eight years old, and I was one of the assistant coaches. After one of the games, we got in the car and Andrew said:

“Dad, your job as coach is not just to tell us what we are doing wrong. Your job is to inspire us!”

What a lesson I learned that day. That is exactly your job as a management person, a parent, a person. What a difference it makes!

Always Shortstop

Throughout all Little League baseball, Andrew just loved, loved, loved playing. He was always determined to excel and was frequently written off from playing shortstop because of his size. That was before the coach watched him play. Whether five years old or 15 years old, he was just an outstanding infielder.

At about five years old, after Andrew threw someone out from the shortstop position, his first Little League coach, Bill Sigler, said, "You got a gun, Andrew; you've got a gun."

Andrew was selected for the All Stars. Although the extended family was going on a great vacation, he stayed home to play baseball. Players from every team made up the team. After surveying the team, the coach said to me, "He's probably not going to be my starting shortstop." He was! After all of the practicing, the coach realized that Andrew was making the greatest plays and making the fewest errors. He was also great at hitting and usually was the leadoff hitter. He never was the home run hitter, but certainly was good at getting on base, whether getting hits or having a keen eye for the strike zone and getting walks.

When not playing shortstop, Andrew was a pitcher. In high school, his playing ended, but what a learning experience he had playing the game that he loved!

Walk Off Home Run

While playing baseball in the semi-final game of the year, we were playing one of the best teams in the league. They were expected to beat us and play the other best team for the championship. They were beating us by one run in the bottom of the ninth inning.

We had a player on base and Alex was coming up to bat. The assistant coach of the other team told his coach, "I wouldn't pitch to Alex." The other coach said, "I'll pitch to him." On the first pitch, Alex knocked it out of the park and over the fence. Walk off home run!!

Though Alex would hit many more home runs, that was one of my favorites of the greatest hits of his career!

Why Throw a Strike?

When Alex was pitching in Little League, he threw a strike that was hit for a home run, then the coach yelled, "Why did you throw him a strike over the plate?" Alex's response was priceless when he said, "It's Over!!!"

It's out of here! (Spring 2006)

Three Lovely Daughters Picture

While dating my future wife, Nita Day, I was to meet her mom for the first time. We entered the home and Nita introduced me, and after the usual exchange of greetings, I noticed a 30x36 oil painting of her "four" daughters on the wall.

Thinking I was being nice, I said, "Three lovely daughters...you must be very proud!" (Long silence). Nita said, "THREE?" I immediately could hear myself in my head saying three.

Needless to say, that was embarrassing and only because of Nita's love for me did we overcome that. The picture famously became known as the picture of "Three Lovely Daughters!"

We have now been married for 40+ years and I still am harassed by all concerning which one isn't lovely. I weakly tried to explain by saying that I meant three lovely sisters. You can guess how successful that was! Love overcomes all, and it would be impossible to explain how much I love all of the four lovely daughters of the Day clan and feel very loved by them.

All four of the "three lovely daughters." Nita and sisters Grace, Debbie, and Jo. Oops! (July 1979)

Parents' Wedding

My parents were married at an early age on October 22, 1936. The wedding had to be delayed until my mother became 17 years old, which in those days was the earliest a woman could marry. My mother's birthday was September 25th and they married soon after that.

My dad will not turn 21 until the following December. He always said, "I was never my own boss. My mother was my boss until I could become an adult at 21 years of age and before that, I married your mom, and she became my boss."

I'm not sure that anyone "bossed" my dad about anything, but it made a good story, and he was all for that!

Wedding Party: Erma Albritton Chelette, pianist; Roy A. Anderson, father of the bride; C.T. Lewis, best man; James O. Albritton, groom; Elisabeth E. Anderson, bride; Doris Anderson, maid of honor; and Patricia Mann, flower girl. (October 22, 1935)

False Teeth Wisdom

My dad reached the point of having to obtain false teeth plates. The dentist at the consultation appointment discussed all of the wonderful improvements possible, and how he could make the new teeth look perfect.

After listening to all of the details and suggestions, my dad said that he wanted the teeth made exactly like his existing ones so that he would continue to look exactly like the same person.

The dentist finally agreed and after all was done, my dad looked exactly the same and you could not even tell that he was wearing dentures.

Many of the old-timers knew way more than most of us gave them credit for! What a lesson from my dad to love yourself as you are!

April Fool's Joke

While I have never been good at pulling these types of jokes on people, I was successful on one occasion with Nita. We were on the way to the airport in Orlando for a flight to San Francisco. It just happened to be April Fool's Day and nothing had been said about that. As we were driving on the interstate highway, I told Nita that the car wasn't driving right and pulled to the edge of the busy highway. We each got out to check the tires on our side. She said all was good on her side and I said "Oh no, we have a flat over here." We either had to change the tire or wait for AAA and hope to still make the flight! She was so unhappy until I said, "April Fool!" Then she was mad! No, she really laughed, we made the flight, and had a wonderful time!

Christi & the Queen of England

In the summer of 1979, my seven-year-old daughter Christi, her mother, and I took a trip to Spain for vacation. Since I only had two weeks of vacation, I had to return to work. Since her mom was a teacher and was off for the summer, the decision was made for Christi and her mom to continue the vacation in England before flying home.

After they returned home, Christi wrote the following letter to the Queen of England:

> "Your highness, I have been to the country you rule and it is beautiful. I am 7 and from the U.S.A."

Several weeks later we were surprised when she received a response from the queen's Lady-in-Waiting postmarked at Balmoral Castle. The letter was dated September 6, 1979, on Buckingham Palace letterhead and said:

> "Dear Christina.
>
> I am commanded by The Queen to write and thank you for your letter.
>
> Her Majesty thought it was so nice of you to write as you did, and I am to send you The Queen's sincere thanks for your kind thought in doing so."
>
> Sincerely,
> Lady-in-Waiting

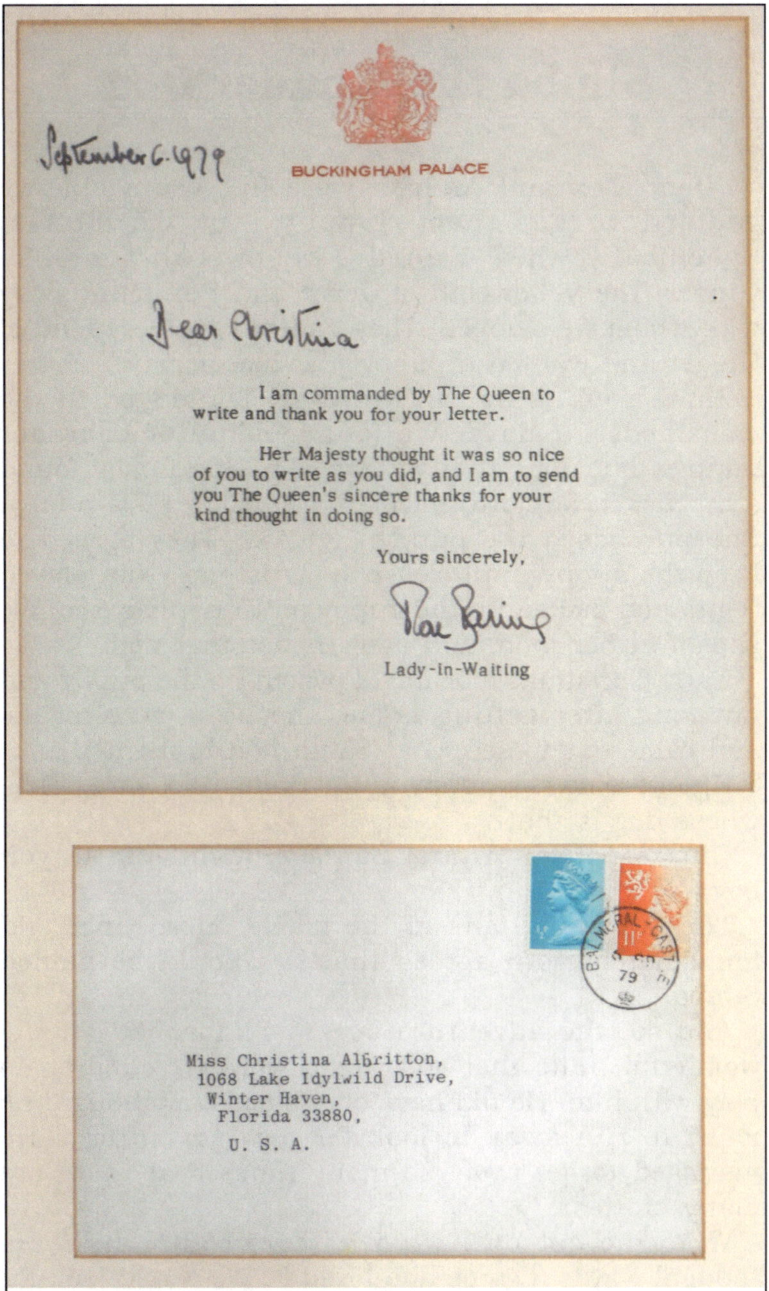

September 6. 1979

BUCKINGHAM PALACE

Dear Christina

I am commanded by The Queen to write and thank you for your letter.

Her Majesty thought it was so nice of you to write as you did, and I am to send you The Queen's sincere thanks for your kind thought in doing so.

Yours sincerely,

Lady-in-Waiting

Miss Christina Albritton,
1068 Lake Idylwild Drive,
Winter Haven,
Florida 33880,
U. S. A.

Queen's response to letter from Christi (age 7) after visiting England. (September 6, 1979)

Simba the Wonder Dog

When Alex and Andrew were five years old, we decided to get them a puppy for Christmas. Specifically, they wanted a yellow Labrador like Ginger, the yellow lab of Jerry and Bev Dunnaway with whom we camped. They had become very fond of Ginger and wanted a puppy just like her.

Santa's job is not always easy! We looked in the classifieds for days. We found plenty of Labrador puppies but none that were yellow. Nita finally found a breeder in Sanford that had one yellow male puppy. She purchased the puppy that day. They agreed to keep the puppy until closer to Christmas. Nita played Santa and picked up the puppy on Christmas Eve. We kept it at her mom and dad's house that night.

Early Christmas morning, I picked up the puppy and not long after getting home, the boys were awake and came out to see what Santa had brought them.

Upon seeing the puppy in the crate, Alex said, "Hey, whose dog is that?"

Our response: "Yours! Santa brought him to you boys!"

They were big fans of the movie, Lion King, and immediately both agreed that he should be named Simba!

And so, the adventure began. Simba had all the wonderful traits that you would want for children to play with him. He did have one major flaw though: he loved to run away to look for new adventures! He managed to get away so many times that there are many stories.

When he got out, we always ran after him. He thought it was a game and loved it. We would look for him with the car and finally find him in the backyard of someone's house. The problem was that as soon as he saw us, the game was on again, and off he went. He would willingly let anyone else grab him but not the game players (the family).

While Nita was looking for him one day in the neighborhood, she was driving down Trinity Circle, a street across from our house. She saw a lady in the neighborhood who said, "That is just dangerous! Walking your dog that way."

Nita explained, "I'm not walking him, I'm trying to catch him."

By then, Simba had bolted down the street with Nita in pursuit!

He got out another day and we could not find him anywhere in the neighborhood. Our fear was that he might try to cross Havendale Boulevard, which is a six-lane busy highway that is only 3 houses away. He had never run in that direction, but we were getting desperate. Nita had to take the boys to school without knowing where he was, and I was at work. She called the county animal control, but they had no record of picking up a yellow lab.

We found out later that he had in fact crossed the six-lane highway without getting hit and had ended up at Westwood Middle School over 2 miles away from our home. He was so friendly that he went straight into the school cafeteria with the school kids! They were having a blast petting Simba and giving him food. The teachers and cafeteria workers were much less happy about the situation and called animal control. We were finally able to talk to them and found out that the dog catcher had him in the truck with the other dogs they had picked up. We met her at the end of her workday, and again had our favorite dog, Simba!

Simba was always very strong, and while trying to walk him on a leash, he always wanted to go faster than you were going. While we were camping in Okeechobee, I decided to take Simba for a walk on his leash. I decided to ride Nita's bike on the gravel road and looped the leash around the handlebars of the bike. The leash line would extend so that Simba could run beside me in the grass. All was going well until Simba suddenly saw a rabbit. He broke toward the rabbit at a full run, yanking the leash free of the bike and causing me to crash onto the gravel road. The rabbit escaped and I retrieved Simba but as the saying goes, "I was not a happy camper!"

When Alex was very young, he was walking Simba with a leash at Southport campground. Simba saw an animal and pulled so hard that he pulled Alex face down and dragged him through the mud. Alex has always been a very strong and determined person, and I am sure he hung onto the leash, but at that time he wasn't happy with his beloved dog, Simba.

It is a wonder that Simba survived with us, partly because of our frustrations with his running away, and partly because of the danger of him getting hit by a car. Alex saw him get hit slightly on his rear end, but he bounced up and was off again. He never chased cars, but I think getting hit made him more aware to stay away from cars. Many more things happened with Simba, some of which are in our camping stories.

Simba's health became quite worse in his old age and some of us were considering whether we should have him put down. He became quite feeble and could hardly get up. Loving them so much makes it so hard! While he was sleeping close to the glass doors, Nita saw a buzzard come up to the glass and look at him. The buzzard left and came back with a second buzzard. Simba was still alive and still his normal self for this stage of his life, but we interpreted that to mean "it is time." We made the difficult decision and contacted our vet.

We all made the trip to the vet, but the boys just could not go in. Nita and I went in, but we were all there for Simba. The fun times with Simba came to an end, but the memories will last forever!!

Ready to go... anywhere and fast! (Fall 2000)

Ice Breaker

The first speech in Toastmasters is called an ice-breaker speech. Since it is your first speech, it is supposed to be about you. I decided to begin my speech by indicating that I was just a country boy. I opened by quoting the words of the "perfect country and western song" that was frequently playing on pop radio.

As I stood at the microphone nervously, the first words coming out of my mouth were as follows:

> "I was drunk the day my mom got out of prison (pause)
> And I went to pick her up in the rain (pause with crowd chuckles)
> And before I could get there in my pickup truck (more chuckles)
> She got run over by a damned ole train."

Well, I went on with my speech and after it was over, a friend came up explaining how upset she was. She thought all of it was true and was upset that the audience was laughing. In the speech, I was able to achieve my purpose of helping the audience understand that I am just a country boy who likes to have fun. I may not be successful in financial riches, but I am in having fun! Happily, that continues.

Dunking Tank

Our company was celebrating being in the community for 20 years with an outside event. One of the fun activities was a dunking tank and I was one of the management volunteers to be the clown sitting on the trap door. All of the employees had a blast trying to dunk the boss in the water—especially my employees! Only a few were accurate enough to dunk me into the water but then they got my boss to throw. He, Tom McCrone, was an ex-Minor League Baseball player. He was very accurate with his throws and my employees insisted that he keep pitching. Many dunks later, you could say that they had a ball...and to a large degree, so did I, only wetter!

Fun but wet!! (1982)

The Magician and Jokester

One of my employees, Horace, was quite good as a magician and liked to pull pranks on people. It always amazed me that without any preplanning, people would help him.

One of his pranks occurred when I was introducing a new employee, Holly. As usual, I walked around to each employee's desk with the newly hired person and told each of them the name of the other.

As Holly and I walked up to Horace's desk, he began using sign language with her. The implication, of course, was that Horace couldn't speak.

I then asked Holly, "You are able to do sign language, right?"

The look of horror on her face quickly vanished when he and I burst into laughter. Luckily, Holly had a great sense of humor and turned out to be a great employee even though she had to put up with Horace.

He saw another one of my employees (Keitha) away from work in a retail store. She didn't see him, and he made his way behind her, stuck his finger in her back and said, "Stick 'em up!" She did and while holding her hands over her head, he then said, "Now turn around very slowly." She did, and when she recognized him, she started hitting him with her purse! Some cop would have shot me.

The pranks were not limited to my employees. Everyone wanted to win the lottery and he bought a ticket. In the early days, you checked if you had won by comparing your ticket to the winning numbers posted in the newspaper. Horace handed his lottery ticket to a woman friend of his and asked her to check the numbers while he read the winning numbers from the paper. What she didn't know was that Horace had written the numbers on the ticket in the paper that he was reading from. As he read the numbers, her "Yes" got louder and more excited as he read. After the last number was read, she jumped up and hugged his neck while yelling, "You won...you won!" After she found out the truth, she too was beating on him.

As a magician, Horace had many tricks that mesmerized people and frightened some. One of my favorites was the "floating dollar bill." He would ask someone for a dollar bill, crush it into a ball, hold it out in front of him, and let go with his hands, leaving it to float in the air. It would sometimes go up and down. The religious people in the room thought that he was "possessed by the devil" and were afraid to be near him.

My last magician story involves a management meeting that we were having, in which he made the division manager disappear. Unfortunately, it was only temporary! Actually, the boss was a great guy and he came back!

Horace started as an employee that I hired and eventually became a fellow supervisor, a great fishing buddy, and a dear friend.

Speechless Twice

All my employees gathered around my desk to wish me a Happy Birthday. I was sitting down. One of the employees, Joan, suddenly jumped on my lap giving me a big hug, and just sat there! I was speechless!!

The second time occurred when I was a young management person, and an employee asked for a meeting with me in the conference room. When I entered the conference room, she was already there and the first thing she said was, "I am in love with you!" I was speechless!!

I finally uttered some senseless phrases about women falling in love with their doctors and supervisors, but that I wasn't in love with her and hoped that it wouldn't affect her working for me. I also was terrified that the other employees might find out. As far as I know, no one did, but years later when I told someone the story they almost died of curiosity because I wouldn't divulge the person's name.

Santa Hats

I was asked to be an emcee at the Division Christmas Party along with my friend and fishing buddy, Horace West. We both were to wear Santa hats. When I arrived at the meeting, Horace had placed a cone inside his hat which made it stand up. My hat was floppy.

I said into the mike, "That's the difference between youth and old age."

The laughter certainly got the meeting off to a fun start!

Credit Union Gifts

The annual meeting of the State Farm Federal Credit Union always involved a lot of financial and statistical information presented to the group. George Wise, manager of the credit union as well as the Board of Directors decided that gifts should always be given away as an enticement for increased attendance and to make sure that we had the required number of attendees for a quorum.

Numbers were given out as each member entered, and a copy of that number dropped in the gift drawing bowl. George and I were very good friends, so guess who was designated as the person to describe the gift and announce the winning number? If you had the winning number drawn, you won the specific gift that I described.

After making fun of the gift and describing the type of person who would or would not like the gift, the number was drawn, and I announced the winning number. It turned out more like a comedy routine than a boring gift drawing, and attendance at the meeting was definitely high.

As an example of my comments prior to the number being drawn, I was giving away a male hair care combo kit. I said something crazy like "This next gift must really be appropriate for the male person most vain about his appearance." I then said, "I hope to god that no one from the executive office has this number." Everyone laughed. The number drawn was handed to me and I called the number! The executive office did not win, but the winner was most definitely the male person in the building most particular about his appearance. The crowd roared with laughter!

After the first time that I gave away the gifts, the meetings were always handled that way and there was no way that George was interested in me getting released from that job. Great fun was had by all and we had wonderful meetings!

Always laughter at my description of the items given away for the gift drawing.

How to Make a Peanut Butter Sandwich

As a management person for a large insurance company, I was asked to teach a letter-writing class about responding to complaints from policyholders and the Florida Insurance Department. I assigned homework prior to the class. Each employee attending was to write a letter explaining how to make a peanut butter sandwich and send it to me. My wife had been given this assignment in college.

After reading their letters of instruction before class, I planned to follow their instructions exactly as written to demonstrate that we sometimes aren't clear in our written communications. I came prepared with utensils, a pan, the necessary ingredients, etc. Some of the written instructions:

- Put a nice sized "blob" of peanut butter on one piece of bread and a "blob" of jelly on the other and put together facing inward.

I put a blob on each with my fingers since there were no instructions to use a knife. Also, there was no indication to open either of the jars or to spread them on the piece of bread.

- Before eating, cut the sandwich into quarters so as not to offend Emily Post. Here's how: With a large, sharp, serrated knife, slice the sandwich diagonally from top right to bottom left. Rotate the cutting board 180 degrees and repeat the cutting process. Gently remove the four sections to a serving plate.

It is still in diagonal halves! You cut the same place as the first cut!

- For an even more enjoyable sandwich, add one large glass of lemonade. If that's not the best sandwich following the exact recipe, see me. Signed, Peanut Butter Sandwich Specialist!

I poured the large glass of lemonade onto the sandwich (now in a pan) which made it pretty soggy! I said to the class, "Give yourselves a hand. I think you all now qualify as Peanut Butter Sandwich Specialists."

I had the acknowledgment of all that we could improve our letter-writing skills and had created a fun learning environment at the same time.

Debi—Practical Joke

Debi locked my computer screen as a practical joke, knowing that I would have to ask her for help in unlocking it. She and Chris Sheffield were to be trainers on new computer changes. Her plan would have worked except another one of my employees, Cameron Kelpsa, tipped me off about her plan.

I went to Chris and told him to call Debi and say: "I don't know what got into Art, but he found out what you are doing with his password and locking his screen. He came to my desk, and he was really hot. He said that if you can't take your trainer responsibilities seriously, maybe he should get someone else. Anyway, I just wanted you to know."

As I walked by Debi's desk, she was on the phone. I knocked on her desk with my knuckles and said, "When you get off the phone I need to see you."

When she walked up to my desk, obviously upset, I looked up at her and said "Gotcha" and laughed.

Relieved, she laughed too, but never tried to trick me again!

Seminar Planning with Linda

I was frequently asked to be involved in the planning and emceeing of seminars, especially when Linda was in charge of the event. Our division had three management people one step above my position, and one of those people was always assigned to oversee the seminar. Linda frequently asked me to be on the planning team because together we always made the event fun, and everyone loved those seminars.

Two examples of Linda's creativity come to mind. I'm not sure where the original idea came from, but she was creative in its use. For one of the events, she asked each of the management attendees to submit one interesting thing about themselves to the department secretary that would make the other attendees say, "I didn't know that." It could be about a hobby, a trip they took, something they did as a child, and it could be serious or funny. It should be short and a maximum of only one sentence. It was our secret until the meeting where it would be shared.

We took the information that each told us about themselves and added three other things as possibilities that could be the one provided by each individual. At the seminar, we read the individual's name followed by the four possible answers. All the individuals attending then decided which of the four answers was the one provided by the individual named. Some of the options added were funny for that person and were frequently picked as the one provided.

It was fun and generated lots of laughter. It helped everyone get to know each other better, was a wonderful icebreaker, and everyone loved it! It was a great beginning that created a lasting positive attitude throughout the seminar!

The second example was a management meeting where our theme was "Creating Solutions." Relating to that theme, we created a "Creating Solutions Listing of Resources." It was like a scavenger hunt listing. We divided the group into three teams of participants sitting near each other. The instructions were: "Without leaving the room, the goal is to obtain as many of these items as possible and place them in the middle of the table. You may begin. You have nine minutes. Of the 66 possible items, Team A got 54, Team B got 32 and Team C got 41!"

The follow-up was extremely interesting as it related to the theme of the meeting, "Creating Solutions." Let me summarize with the questions that I asked the group:

1. Did your team utilize all available resources for "creating solutions?"
2. Can anyone think of a way that your team could have gotten more of the resources listed but your team wouldn't listen to you?
3. Did all of you get all the resources that you could possibly get?
4. Did you ask members of other teams for items? Why not?
5. Did any of the rules say that this was a competition between teams?
6. Within the stated rules, were there any more possibilities for "creating solutions?"
7. Did anyone consider asking a non-team member to leave the room to get resource items for your team?
8. Did anyone consider asking Linda or me? Between us, we have almost every single item.
9. Did anyone interpret the goal as getting more than one of each item? "The goal is to obtain as many of these resources as possible."

The obvious lesson is that we **must** be alert to **all** possibilities for "creating solutions."

I am very thankful for my work opportunities with Linda. We were able to make learning fun for others and had a great time doing it!

Gift Dropping

When I was a freshman in college at the University of South Florida, I was dating a senior at Lake Wales High School. She was very pretty and it was early in a dating experience, but I decided to get her a gift for Christmas.

I had heard about a prank involving a gift box with broken glass in it. When giving it to her, you would release the box just before she has her hands on it. I'm not sure what it says about my personality, but I decided to try it. Timing is everything!

Just before her hands touched the box, I released it. Falling to the floor and upon impact, it sounded like the delicate gift was destroyed! She cried, I felt like an idiot, and for some consolation, I had a nice string of pearls for her in my coat pocket.

P.S. I don't recommend trying this, especially on your wife!

Talking Christmas Tree

Every year during the Christmas season, we would have a division meeting for our division manager, Barry Thomas, to give us an update on our performance for reaching division goals. He wanted the meeting to be a festive and fun event and selected me to be in charge of planning the meetings.

For one meeting, I decided to arrange for part of the decorations to include a Talking Christmas Tree. I had been listening to radio station Q105 and they were describing how hilarious it is to wire it into a sound system without the speaker knowing. I had to try this! I found one of the trees which looks like a regular Christmas tree until activated when the eyes and mouth move in sync to the sound. I then used the tree for decoration and had it wired to the podium microphone and sound system. No sound was sent to the tree while all of us were using the podium mike.

Now it was time for our division manager, Barry Thomas, to address the group! I turned the sound system so that everything he said would go to the Talking Christmas Tree, which would mimic everything he said live.

Barry said, “Good afternoon.”

The tree was off to the side and ahead of him, so he saw nothing, but the audience roared with laughter. He walked out and looked at the tree which everyone was obviously looking at. Everything looked normal as soon as the mouth and eyes closed.

He walked back to the mike and said, “Let’s try this again. Good afternoon.”

The audience goes wild with laughter again!

I then had Barry stand in the audience while I went to the microphone and said, "Good afternoon." Everyone laughed, including Barry, and for my job security, I assured him that I was turning it off. What fun, exciting meetings, and how thankful we were to have such a great boss!

Training Wheels

Andrew decided that he was going to learn to ride his bike without using training wheels. The challenge was made even more difficult because he decided while we were on a camping trip to Southport on Lake Toho, and the campground road was made of crushed rock.

Andrew was determined and wanted "no help" from any of us. The experience as I remember it was ride and fall, ride and fall, ride and fall, and bandage Andrew's scrapes and bruises. Repeat, repeat, repeat. Finally, I adjusted the seat a little lower, he rode away without falling, and he was so proud that he had done it on his own.

Wow, guess he proved to us all again that through hard work it can be done!

Mentoring Debi Evans

State Farm decided to start a Regional Underwriter Training (RUT) program. The plan was to select underwriting trainees from existing service personnel in the auto and fire insurance departments and have them spend the first six months training in the department that they were currently in, and then switch them to the other department for six months of additional training. Then they would be assigned to either of the departments to begin working.

Debi was working in auto and spent the first part of her training there. She then came to the fire company for the second half of her training. My upper management decided that she would be assigned to my team for her training. I selected one of my experienced underwriters, Cameron Kelpsa, to be her trainer. I sat in the back cubicle of one row of my employees, and Debi and her trainer sat one row over to my right. In Debi's words to me (much later), "You never spoke to me for months other than to say good morning." From my point of view, that was quite an exaggeration, but if things were going well, I did try to let things continue.

As the end of her training time was approaching, Debi was certain that she would return to auto for her ultimate destination since she was so much more knowledgeable about auto with her time there. However, her trainer had kept me informed about her progress, how bright she was, and how quickly she learned. I decided that I wanted to keep Debi. Now the fight was on because her auto supervisor wanted her back! I do not know how I got the reputation, but it was that I usually won! I did win that battle and Debi was assigned to my team.

It didn't take long for Debi to make an impression. She was bright, willing to learn, and applied herself to any challenge. After gaining some experience, she did have one problem communicating with a particular agent who wanted her fired or transferred to another group of agents. At this point, Debi was an experienced underwriter and I explained to the Agency Manager that she was one of my best underwriters and I was not going to change. We would work it out.

I sent Debi down to visit all the agents in that district with the primary purpose of spending some time in the office of the difficult agent. It turned out that the problem was the office manager of the difficult agent. After she visited with Debi and learned that Debi, like her, was a NASCAR racing fan, the problem vanished. Managing people can be such a problem, but solutions sometimes come from the strangest places. Debi became an amazing underwriter and was my "lead worker" for several years. It is too difficult for words to describe how helpful she was to me.

Lloyd Hines, the supervisor of the team beside me decided to retire. I decided to recommend Debi for a promotion to supervisor of that team. The only problem was that Lloyd's lead worker, Danielle, was recommended by him. He was mentoring and developing his employee for promotion as I was Debi. The battle was on!

My superintendent, Don Allen, along with another superintendent, Linda Davis, were doing the interviewing of these two candidates along with several others. I not only had written my recommendation of Debi for the position but had also hopefully convinced Don that she was unquestionably the best candidate for the position. If he agreed, he would have to convince Linda, and Don wasn't the best at winning. Linda was great at selecting the best person for a position, so I was confident. After all the interviewing was finished, Debi was selected!

Before the announcements were made to everyone, Linda appeared at my desk and said, "Tell me that Debi has a college degree." Other candidates had been told that a degree would help them get into management. I said, "No, she does not have a college degree. It isn't a requirement, only a recommendation." The decision stood even though there were some unhappy candidates. Linda would tell you today that it was the right decision and frequently says to Debi, "You are one of the brightest people I've ever met."

As I knew and expected, Debi became an outstanding management person and still is. Mentoring didn't end with her selection. It was a difficult transition for her during the first year. Sitting side by side as management people, I helped her with many situations, and she continued helping me with many. Everyone knew that the working relationship between us was strong and that we were very supportive of each other. Between her technical knowledge and brightness and my management experience, the rest of the management team knew that winning a battle against us was formidable. Despite that, our division management team all worked well together, had fun, and accomplished our goals.

Mentoring Debi Evans never ended, though sometimes she was mentoring me. The mentoring ended with my retirement, though we had become great friends and will be forever.

Retirement Party

After 38 years with State Farm Insurance Companies, I suddenly decided to retire. My twin boys, Alex and Andrew, were only 10 years old and I had frequently said that I couldn't retire until they finished college. That would not be for 12 more years. The reason for my early decision was that after adding my retirement pension and my social security money and comparing that total to my salary minus all the taxes and deductions, the difference was pretty small. In fact, that difference divided by my work hours meant that I was making less than $1 per hour for working! I enjoyed my job but not that much! I immediately decided to retire.

Before announcing anything at the office, I made a trip over to see my dear friend and coworker, Debi Evans. I knew that my leaving would be very hard for her. Leaving her would also be very hard for me. We had become very close working side by side and were very good friends outside of work with our camping trips.

The retirement policy requires that an employee give the company 60 days advance notice. I was retiring on June 1st so I had to give them notice on April 1st which was April Fool's Day. I was always joking around and knew that no one would believe me when I told them. I went into the office of my boss and told him just before we were to go to our morning management meeting. I also told him that he would have to announce it to the management group in the meeting as I didn't want to become emotional. He made the announcement, and everyone said, "Right, April Fool's." He finally convinced them, and so the process of retirement began.

Final words: "Take This Job and Shove It." (June 1, 2004)

The company always allowed a retirement party in the cafeteria/ patio area on or near the last day that you would work. In my formal request for retirement, I had already reserved the area and indicated to them that I wanted the party emcee to be my friend and fishing buddy, Horace West. I wanted the party to be only fun with no serious comments about me that might cause me to be touched emotionally. Horace did a great job, as did my employees, with skits and comments, and my coworkers with their remarks. Horace asked my wife, Nita, if she had any comments about having me home all of the time. Her one-word response was "Help!" Finally, it was my time to come to the microphone and make some comments.

I had decided to sing the song, "Take This Job & Shove It" and had arranged for the sound person to play Johnny Paycheck singing it as my accompaniment. As I nervously approached the microphone, I said "I only have one thing to say..." (and the song began). I was using a portable microphone and walked around as I sang: "Take this job and shove it! I ain't working here no more! Better not try to stand in my way, 'cause I'm walking out that door! Take this job and shove it! I ain't working here no more!" As I began to sing, the crowd of 100+ all began clapping as I sang. I should add that I am *not* a singer. As I sang the part about walking out the door, I actually headed toward the exit of the room. Debi told me later that she thought that I was gone, thus ending the program. I had not told her about singing the song. I worked my way back to the podium with my mike and gave my farewell speech. It was mostly comedy because of my desire to keep it from getting sentimental. After the retirement party was over, I heard from people for months who said, “That was the best retirement party ever!!”

I missed the people immensely but not the work, and I loved having the extra time to spend with my children and Nita!

Finding Kick & Go

We had a Kick & Go scooter for kids to ride that could be propelled when you kicked down on the back pedal. Kids loved to ride it.

My nephew, Adam Merritt, (about five years old) was visiting and wanted to ride the scooter. He had previously played with it and said, “I know right where it is!” So off he went into the garage to get it.

He soon came back into the house saying that he couldn’t find it. I said, “I thought you said you knew right where it is?”

He said, “I do! I just don’t know which pile it’s under!”

We found it for him and laugh to this day about the incident. Obviously, our garage needed some cleaning and organization—and still does!

Thanksgivings in Auburn

Living in Florida where Nita's parents and two of her three sisters lived, we usually celebrated Thanksgiving in Florida. My favorite Thanksgivings though were when we celebrated in Auburn, Alabama where the third sister, Debbie, lived.

When I was preparing to write about that Thanksgiving, I realized that we had had three celebrations there and they had all blended together.

The first Thanksgiving in Auburn was in 2002. The weather was absolutely perfect! Nita's parents Max and Billie Day were there and most of her sisters and their husbands and children. The larger the number attending, the better the family Thanksgiving. Debbie and Greg have a gorgeous backyard highlighted at Thanksgiving by a blazing red Japanese Maple tree. It was outrageously gorgeous that year. One of Debbie's favorite pictures of her dad, Max, is him in his Auburn shirt with the fiery red maple tree in the background! Two days after Thanksgiving, all the leaves were gone from the tree due to rain or weather changes and Mom was picking up leaves to enjoy the beauty of each one, but for Thanksgiving, it was perfectly beautiful!!

In 2004, we somehow had Thanksgiving again in Auburn. The children of the four daughters were older and could enjoy playing outside. There were so many things to do in the fall weather. Leaves were everywhere and the kids delighted in raking them into huge piles of leaves and then jumping into them! Zip-lining from the corner of the house out into the backyard was a blast too! Sometimes dropping off into the pile of leaves. Even chopping wood was fun. They took turns trying to chop all the way through large pieces of tree trunks. No one wanted to stop chopping if they thought they could finish all the way through it! Of course, the results were for the wonderful fire in the fireplace, where we could enjoy its beauty and warmth.

For Thanksgiving in 2008, we had Thanksgiving in Auburn again. Debbie pitched the invitation by email for all to come in rhyme, and every person attending or not attending responded in rhyme. Space doesn't allow the printing of all the responses to reflect how creative and funny each was, but I will print the invitation just to give you a sample.

> Dear Family,
> Thanksgiving is only a short month away
> And this email has something important to say!
> You are invited to come to our house to eat
> Cause without YOU our holiday just won't be complete!
> We'll laugh and we'll eat and watch football I'm sure
> Although for Auburn's team I'm afraid there's no cure!
> But no matter – it's fall and it's perfect outside!
> We can walk, we can play, or take a bike ride!
> You could sit by the fire and take time to read
> Or Christmas shop with the greatest of speed!
> But whatever we do – we'll all have some fun
> Just being together – our family – as one!
> Think about coming – Thanksgiving is near
> Come if you can – you ALL are so dear!

Everyone began responding immediately and some with four or more responses! It was an exciting beginning to a truly phenomenal Thanksgiving! We did have one huge negative in that we lost Papa Max Day the previous year, but the good memories will last forever! Otherwise, attendance set a record with Mom, all four daughters and their husbands, and all the grandchildren but two able to attend, and several great-grandchildren. Adam's family and Christi's family could not attend but didn't miss out on the rhyming responses! We even pulled our travel trailer to Auburn for additional sleeping and cooking. All our Thanksgivings are wonderful, but this one was exceptional!

A special thanks to Debbie and Greg for hosting the wonderful Thanksgivings in Auburn!!

Kids having a blast in the leaves. (2002)

Church Emergency Fund

My dad was a deacon in the Baptist Church and decided to establish an emergency fund with money donated by him. I don't know all the details, but I do know that if an emergency were to occur, he would have to agree to the release of the emergency fund money.

Some months later, my dad noticed that they were spending more money each month than the income being received. He discussed this with the board of deacons, but the practice continued and the balance in the bank covered the difference.

After a few months, the chairman of the deacons came to my dad one day and said, "We have an emergency and checks are going to bounce! We need you to release some of the emergency funds."

My dad said, "This isn't an emergency, I have been discussing this in board meetings for months. I will not release emergency funds."

The chairman of the board of deacons (who was a doctor) had to use his personal funds to cover the checks. Obviously, the problem was fixed at the next board meeting! I could not have done what my dad did, but lessons were learned!

The Go-Cart

A go-cart was purchased by Richard Evans, and after he rebuilt everything that needed fixing, we took it to my mother's house in Lake Wales for the boys to ride.

At first, we would only let them ride around my mother's property of a few acres. After we got them started, we went into the house and visited with my mom. Alex and Andrew shared well with each other and after one took a spin, they would come back and let the other one go for a ride.

As we were visiting my mom, Alex came into the house and said, "Andrew needs some help." We went outside to check on the situation. While riding, he had gone through some grass about eight inches high and one side of the go-cart had hit a hidden post lying on the ground and turned over. We got the cart back up on all four wheels and off they went again. Richard decided that we would leave the go-cart in Lake Wales so that the boys could ride anytime that we were at my mother's house without him being there.

Since my mother lived out in the country, there were many dirt roads in the area. Richard began bringing his four-wheel gator when we went over so that he and I could ride in it with one boy, while the other was driving the go-cart. Now we could go riding on the dirt roads! That was great fun! The only problem was that on dirt roads the go-cart kicks up loads of dust!! They managed to handle it and we followed along quite a way back!

They spent many days having fun with that go-cart. Another example of one of Richard's toys providing great fun for the boys!!

Jo's Surprise Engagement Ring

I had married Jo's sister, Anita Day Albritton, a few years earlier and Jo was dating Arturo Pagan, affectionately known as "Arty." In business situations, he went by "Art." It wasn't that common of a first name but these two Day girls were married to or dating an "Art." Sometimes it did create some confusion when someone was calling for Art.

We were all together at Mom and Papa Day's home one day when the phone rang. I answered the phone and the caller said, "Is this Art?" to which I replied, "Yes, it is." They said, "This is the jewelry store and we are just calling to let you know that the engagement ring has been sized and is ready for pickup." I said, "Thank you very much, we'll be right down to pick it up. Thank you for calling."

I immediately got Arty into our private conversation, gave him the information, and assured him that his secret was safe with me.

He soon after proposed to Jo, her answer was "yes," and now many years later, they are still happily married! (I think).

The Pagans now reside in Melbourne, Florida, where Arty is a State Farm Agent, and Jo works for a private school helping seniors get into top-notch colleges. They are blessed with two daughters, Allyson and Lydia, and one son, Max. What a wonderful family despite the brother-in-law who learned of the engagement ring before the actual proposal. Thankfully, I didn't mess that up.

The Pool Hall Retrieval

My mom was always very easy-going. I don't remember ever seeing or hearing my mom and dad argue or raise their voices to each other. One night after midnight, my mom awakened all of us kids, loaded us into the car, and drove into town to the local pool hall. My dad loved to play "snooker" pool. I was never told but I believe that the house rule was to be home by midnight. I know that later it was the rule for us kids.

When we got into town and parked near the pool hall, my mom said, "You kids stay in the car!" I should add that in those days, ladies did not go into pool halls.

My mom knocked on the door and told Ernie, the pool hall owner, that she would like to speak to James (my dad). He came to the door and promised her that he would come right home... "as soon as I finish the game I'm playing"—and he did.

Perhaps I am naïve, but I really believe it came down exactly that way...without any shouting. I must admit that I would have liked to have been a fly on the wall nearby. I also would bet that my mom was pissed and bet that my dad knew it. He came straight home and typical of him... "after he finished that game!" As far as I know, he never came home late from the pool hall again.

Going fishing. (2003)

Outboard Motor Fire

My dad heard that the specs (crappie) were biting in a canal near Fellsmere, which is in the middle of nowhere near Yeehaw Junction. His boss had been catching fish there and agreed to loan his boat to us since it was small with a 3HP outboard motor on it. It was perfect for the long trip up the narrow Fellsmere canal. We took an extra can of gas since it only held a small amount of gas. Putting gas into the motor required you to pour it into a small tank from the top of the motor. We launched the boat and went several miles down the canal. When we ran out of gas, my dad unscrewed the gas cap and filled the tank. He overflowed the tank a little and then started the motor.

The outboard motor cranked on the first pull and immediately caught on fire! My dad didn't panic; he unscrewed the motor from the boat and while holding on to the handle, dunked it underwater to put out the fire. He then raised it above the water, and it was still burning. Now he did panic, dropping the outboard motor to the bottom of the canal. The depth of the water was about six to eight feet deep.

We had no paddle and were miles from the highway up the canal. I volunteered to jump over the side of the boat to try to retrieve it. Taking off all my clothes but my underwear, I jumped over the side of the boat and the water temperature was so cold that I never even let go of the side of the boat. My dad was laughing and said that he should never have sent a boy to do a man's job. He proceeded to take off all his clothes but his underwear. He did let go of the boat, paddled around for about five seconds yelling how cold the water was, and climbed back in the boat. Now what?

My dad suggested that we mark the spot, hand-paddle to the side of the canal, and cut down a small bay tree with his "pocketknife." This we did. The plan was to tie some fishing lures with treble hooks onto the tree with fishing line. This we did, then paddled back to the area we had marked as where the outboard motor had been thrown overboard. After a few tries, we hooked on to something and managed to pull it up. It actually was the motor!

My dad said that he had heard that if you take the spark plugs out and dry them off, it sometimes will start. I guess that we had the tools to do that because that is exactly what we tried.

After a few pulls, the motor started and ran. I kid you not! We went directly up the canal, straight to the car! I have no idea if we caught any fish or even did any fishing. I do know that this is a true story and seeing the end of the canal and our car was definitely the happiest moment of the day for us all!

Fishing—Dad Lost

My dad went fishing in Lake Okeechobee with me and my friend, Horace West. We caught lots of specs in the middle of the lake around Bird Island.

The trip was so successful that my dad decided to go a few days later and take my mother with him. I was at State Farm working when I got a call from him on his cell phone. "I am lost in the middle of Lake Okeechobee and can't find my way in." Feeling totally helpless, I called Horace back to my desk for his thoughts. Luckily, my dad did have a compass, and between the two of us, we were able to get him headed in the right direction. Finally, he found one of our familiar landmarks and they got in safely. Whew...

Jim's Boat Dive

While fishing at Lake Pierce with my brother, we were catching speckled perch (crappie). My brother was in the back seat fishing and I was in the front. My fishing buddy, Horace West, was in a different boat nearby. When Jim attempted to step down, he lost his balance, tried to sit down on the side of the boat, and fell backward out of the boat and into the water like a diver going in!

At my retirement party, the event was best described by Horace. As emcee he was to introduce my brother to speak at the party. Horace said, "Our next speaker is Art's brother, Jim Albritton. I don't know what his occupation is but if he were on the Olympics Diving Team, I would have given him a perfect 10 for that dive out of Art's boat! Welcome, Mr. Jim Albritton..."

Fishing and Camping at Kissimmee State Park

On one of my fishing trips, we decided to take my camping trailer and camp at Kissimmee State Park. The participants were one of my usual fishing buddies, Jeff Snyder, and a second person named Warren Glenn. I knew Warren from his coaching a T-ball team that our sons played on. Jeff knew Warren from attending the same church.

When we completed setting up our camper and Warren his tent, we had a great evening telling stories and enjoying the outdoors. The next morning, we headed out onto the lake to do some fishing and hopefully catch some "specs."

The outing was very successful, and we ended up catching 34 fish. We returned to camp, had some lunch, and decided to go back out on the lake to see if we could catch some more. We left the fish that we had caught in our cooler with a tight-fitting lid and planned to clean them along with any additional fish that we caught.

When we returned later that afternoon with more fish, we found that the raccoons had somehow opened the cooler and eaten the eyes out of all the fish. We certainly didn't plan to eat any of them now, so we took the cooler down to the state park basin and dumped them all in.

The next morning when we went down to the basin to go fishing again, the wildlife game warden was there! He said to us, "Look at that, someone wasted all those fish!"

I wanted to tell him that all the eyes had been eaten out by the raccoons and we had thrown them away, but we all felt that silence was the best policy and just agreed with him on someone wasting the fish.

Later on the lake, we all had a good laugh about it. It was our secret! We had a wonderful weekend catching lots of fish and a good time was had by all.

Fishing—Dad Fell In

Dad loved to fish and in his elder years frequently went with me and my friends. On one occasion he went to Middle Lake Hamilton with me and my friend, Horace West. While we were launching the boat, my dad lost his balance on the bank and fell into the water. It was winter and really cold if you were wet.

He called my mom to bring him some dry clothes so that he could change into dry clothes and still go fishing with us. He was so cold that he was shaking uncontrollably. We put him in my car with the heater running on high.

When she arrived, he decided to go home with her! Even for him, it is sometimes better to wait until next time.

Fishing—Lightning

I went on a fishing trip with my fishing buddy, Jeff Snyder. We wanted to fish just below the locks at Lake Toho at night. The specs were really biting there. The only problem was that the locks closed at sunset, so we would not be able to get back to Lake Toho if we launched there.

The plan was to launch the boat at Camp Mack and drive by boat through the canal into Lake Hatchineha, through Hatchineha/Cypress canal into Lake Cypress, and then through Southport canal up to the locks at Lake Toho to fish. We were on our way before dark and the weather was horrible behind us when we looked back. It was so bad that there was no way to turn back. Our only hope was that it would rain out before it got to us. The further we went, the closer it came. We kept going.

By the time that we got to our destination, the lightning was the worst that I have ever experienced. It was cracking so loud and close that we were terrified! We tied the boat to the bank, climbed the bank, and walked a mile down a dirt road to the Lake Toho store. It was open and we huddled there until the horrible storm passed.

We then walked back to our boat. We made it home safely, but never did any fishing that night! I haven't done that again and don't plan to!

Built by the boys driving nails—with a little help. Floorplan drawn by each! (Spring 2001)

The Tree House

When Alex and Andrew were seven years old, they decided that we should build a tree house. We had oak trees in the backyard, and they picked the one that had three main trunks coming out of the ground—a perfect tree for a treehouse. Each created a drawing of how it should be done.

The boys searched the garage for materials, and I purchased any remaining items needed. Then the project work and fun began. If a manual saw was used, boards were sawed by all, and if a power saw was used, I was the only one using it. Each person had a hammer and was responsible for nailing their side of the treehouse.

The tree house was not only to have a floor but also a porch-like railing for safety reasons. Everyone was involved in the project, including mom.

I don't remember how long it took to complete the project, but I do remember how pleased the boys were that they had built their tree house (with a little help from mom and dad). They spent many hours playing in the tree house and even decided to spend the night out there one night. Later in the evening they climbed down the ladder and decided to spend the rest of the night in the house snuggled in their own beds.

It was fun and used for several years. When they lost interest, and it began to deteriorate, it was time to take it down. That too was fun as we listened to them remember and tell stories about time in the tree house.

Mother's Almost Bankruptcy

My phone rang on July 19, 2001, and the call was from my brother, James David. His opening words were, "We have a serious financial problem concerning the family groves!" I had not been involved at all in the groves since I had my own career. He had been advised by Farm Credit and the banks that they would not loan any more money, but it was needed to pay off debt and grow next year's crop. The normal plan is to pay off the loans when next year's crop is picked but times had evidently been getting harder and harder.

A financial analysis and plan for action was immediately required. The results showed that the value of the three groves, our mother's house, and all the grove equipment might be adequate for clearing all of the loans and mortgages. David asked my mother what her decision would be if we had to

Sad process but achieved our goal. (January 26, 2002)

decide between keeping some of the groves for income or keeping the family home. She immediately said keeping her home. The next step was selling the groves and grove equipment. The problem was that there was no market for selling orange groves at that time.

The next decision was to auction off the groves and equipment. We contacted Randy Kincaid Auction and he agreed to handle the auction for us. What a difficult decision to make and to be there while the auction took place. My dad was deceased, but it was somewhat emotional to get rid of everything he had worked for. My mother, two brothers, and sister all did well emotionally through it all.

Just prior to the auction beginning, the auctioneer got an offer for the three groves that we accepted. Everything else was then sold.

We accomplished our goal, and the family home was saved! Mother was so happy!

JOA Jobs

My dad was always a hard worker and worked one job in town as a bookkeeper and a second job tending to his orange groves in Lake Wales. There was always more to be done in the groves than could be accomplished. After the boys were grown and my dad retired from his day job, he did most of the grove work.

When my dad saw something that needed to be done, he could not help but begin trying to do it. It didn't matter that he was currently involved in a different job, he would switch to the new job...temporarily! These side jobs became known as "JOA jobs!" That was true for all of us and continues. He's been gone for 26 years.

Nita was recently talking to her sister, Debbie, who was involved in a project at her house in Auburn. Debbie said, "I then got sidetracked in a JOA job." So, the legend of the James O. Albritton side jobs continues. It happens a lot in my family, especially among us boys, and it has extended to Nita's family and probably beyond.

Life is full of interesting stories and anecdotes. We just need to take the time to remember them and help them live on.

Swing Set Assembly

When my daughter, Christi, was very young, we decided to get her a swing set for Christmas. Her grandfather, Buddy Tison, was very handy putting things together and we were certain that we were up to the task on Christmas Eve. As fate would have it, Buddy became ill and was in the hospital. Now it was up to a young Art to complete the task for Santa on Christmas Eve.

As everyone knows, work usually cannot begin until the child is asleep in bed. However, because the task was considered "challenging," we began early in the garage around 8 p.m. with her mom preventing her from coming out.

As a young person you haven't acquired as many tools as you acquire over the years, but hoping for an adequate amount, hoping for clear instructions, and hoping for sufficient intelligence to understand them, the work begins.

After many hours of work in my garage, it was finally beginning to look like a swing set, and all that needed to be done to finish was put two pieces together for the feet to rest on for a back-and-forth swing. Since the two pieces wouldn't fit, something was wrong. I finally figured out that the two pieces at the top of the slide went here and these went at the top of the slide. Words cannot express my thoughts, and if they could, they would be bleeped.

Finally, the swing set was completed at around 1 a.m. Due to the early beginning in the garage, I had failed to consider two important details.

First, how do I get it out under the garage door?!

Secondly, how do I carry this thing around the house to put it on the back patio by the glass doors for her to see where Santa left it!

Somehow the tasks were completed, and we had a very merry Christmas!

Sinking Boat with John Guilfoile

We were fishing in the middle of Lake Kissimmee and must have hit something in the water because suddenly the boat began filling up with water. John Guilfoile and I were near Bird Island and made our way into shallow water. We bailed water out of the boat for 30 minutes to an hour and got it empty. The plan was to run all the way in without stopping. Usually, it doesn't take on water while you are running. We started out, and about halfway to Rabbit Island, which was on the way in, the boat was full of water again.

Luckily, it was not sinking below a certain level. By now, we certainly had our life jackets on, and the outboard motor would run so we decided to try to get in. With John sitting as far as possible up front, I could run the motor at a speed that the water was going over the back of the boat at the same rate that the water was coming in. It took a while to get in, but we made it. We found the hole that had been knocked in the boat bottom. Mostly we were just happy to be safely back.

Horseback Riding

by Christi Albritton Bass

As a little girl, I loved horses. My dad's dad had a pinto pony named Dolly, her brown and white splotches uniformly spread over her stocky body. In one of my earliest memories, I was lifted up and placed on her back. She was pull-reined—at least, that's the term I remember. To get her to turn, we would tug on either the left rein or the right one. She was the most mild-mannered pony I've ever met; I don't remember there being any wildness in her at all as she'd patiently let my cousins and I ride her around the front yard of my grandparents' house.

Later, when I was six, I got my own pony. I vaguely remember going to a place and riding her in a ring, and then the woman who was selling her having second thoughts because her daughter would be too upset by the sale. I remember crying myself. My mom talked to the woman, and long story short, I had myself a horse at the end of the day.

The pony previously had three different names: Lightning, Dusty, and something else I can't remember. I decided to rename her Dusty. I had a little black saddle with a matching black bridle. Dusty was neck-reined, and I rode Western-style. I would lift myself up onto her like a pro—always approaching from the left side, placing my booted or sneakered foot in the little stirrup and swinging myself over her back, then settling atop her and pressing my legs against her sides. And then we were off! I rode that pony hard, and she had some spirit. I cantered or ran her as much as possible, reluctantly slowing to a walk only when sweat was covering both of us.

The house I actually lived in was in the suburbs, on a lake, but the horses and Dusty were kept in a stable and field owned by my great-grandmother, not far

It began with the pony. (1978)

from my grandparents' house. My parents paid a man named Bob, a distant relative, to take care of them.

This was before my parents got divorced, and each of them had horses. Before I had Dusty, my mom had a quarter-horse chestnut mare named Yankee, and my dad had a large brown horse named Poco. Both horses were very gentle. I remember going into the stalls with them as a little girl, pressing my face against their necks or withers and just breathing in the horsey scent of them. Since I didn't have my own horse at the time, I would ride behind either one parent or the other, my small arms wrapped around their waists. Something happened to Poco: I don't remember if he was ill, or if my dad just wanted a horse with a little more spirit—but he disappeared, and we got Ali. Ali was—fittingly—an Arabian horse, white, with a pretty dished face and a long, windswept blackish-gray mane. Ali was spirited enough to make me a little nervous, swishy and prone to spook or shy, though he never bit or kicked. I was comfortable sitting on Yankee and holding the reins by myself, but I didn't want to sit on Ali unless my dad was with me.

After I had Dusty, the three of us would ride all around the area, through the orange groves where my dad had grown up, some of the groves belonging to my grandfather. When we'd take a break, to let the horses rest, my dad would pick oranges for us to eat. He knew I didn't like the pulp, so he would methodically take off the outside peel with his pocket knife, carving a cone-shaped opening into the top of the fruit. He taught me how to squeeze the sides so that the opening would fill with juice. In that way, I could drink fresh orange juice, right off the tree, as the hot Florida sun beat down over us. I wish I could still remember what truly fresh-squeezed juice tasted like. I remember the subsequent stickiness of the juice drying onto my fingers. I guess when I had finished, we tossed my little makeshift cup with its seeds back into the grove, or into some surrounding grass.

I got thrown lots of times. I think once I got thrown while on back of Ali, probably because something made him glance away to the side, and for whatever reason either I couldn't hold onto my dad or he wasn't on Ali at the time. Falling off the horses was scary for me because they were so high up off the ground. I know at times Dusty, like most ponies, bucked or reared or tried to unseat me. I was a good rider, but sometimes I still got tossed. When that happened, someone would dust me off, and then both of my parents would tell me to get back up and get on that horse, sometimes forcefully. For me, "getting back up on the horse" was a literal fact of life instead of metaphor, but it's still a lesson that served me well in the years that followed.

After my parents got divorced, the stable was one part of my life that stayed the same, although now we had two riders instead of three. My mom kept Yankee, but at another stable, and I don't think she rode at all during that time. I didn't live with her, so I didn't know. I remember riding in my dad's big yellow truck to the stable on Saturday. Frequently, he'd stop at a convenience store to get gas and buy me a honey bun and some chocolate milk to eat for breakfast. I loved those times. Oddly enough, I don't know if my dad still rode at that point. My memory of Ali just fades away, but I still remember riding Dusty. And then eventually the unthinkable happened: Dusty got founder. Founder is a severe hoof disease that horses sometimes get. Once they have it, they are unable to be ridden, because it's incredibly painful for them. We made arrangements for Dusty to be sold to "a nice family that wasn't going to ride her." Many years later, as an adult, I just assumed that she was put down and my dad hadn't wanted to tell me. At that time, as a child, I still believed in a nice family, but I was also sad. I didn't quite understand why she couldn't stay with me. I hopped up on her back and took her for one last ride. I cannot believe that pony didn't try to throw me, given the status of her feet, but she didn't. Maybe she knew, too. Anyway, my dad was upset with me when I returned, explaining in no uncertain terms that what I'd done was wrong. I don't remember getting into big trouble for it, though. I think maybe my dad understood too.

Much later, I would return to riding again, only this time it was with my mom and not my dad. Yankee lived a long time, and as a teenager I would throw a bridle on her, hop on her without a saddle, and canter through the field at the stable where my mom kept her. Still, those times were sporadic and all too short. By the time I was 18, I had stopped riding altogether. That said, even now at age 52 I'm much more comfortable in jeans than dresses or skirts or cute outfits. I love animals, all animals, profoundly, and I don't eat meat. I know no matter what happens, I can push forward and do what's brave. And I'm so absurdly grateful, particularly to my dad and dad's parents, for having the privilege to ride horses as a child.

Edwin—Making New Friends

My Uncle Edwin decided that it was too lonely living in his home after his wife died and decided to move into a relatively new assisted living place in Lake Wales. The place was big and already had a large number of residents. Since he had lived in Lake Wales most of his life, he knew more than half of the residents. Sometime later, his health wasn't quite as good, and he considered moving to an assisted living place that provided greater service. It was in Lakeland where he would not know anyone.

My brother said to Edwin, "What about leaving all the friends that you know here?"

Edwin's answer was priceless! He said, "Then I will make new friends!"

Wow! At his age he was that confident in doing that. He would have been able to do it too! He ended up not moving. He decided that it wasn't necessary for the extra care. He was also so active where he was. After he turned ninety, he formed the "Over 90's" group that met weekly.

He was also still fishing. He had taken me fishing many times when he was younger. Now it was my time to take him. When I would drive to the assisted living place, he would be sitting outside with his two fishing poles and ready to go. We were still doing this when he was 90 years old! He finally fell and broke something, and his fishing days were over.

What an inspiration he was to everyone, especially to me.

The boys with our friends and fellow campers Richard, Debi, and Kelly Evans. (Summer 2003)

Camping at Southport

Our favorite place for camping was always Southport Park located on Lake Toho. It was the place of more memories and stories than any other place that I can remember. The reason that it was our favorite place to camp was that we had many friends who camped there with us. Always Richard & Debi Evans with their daughter, Kelly and frequently Bev & Jerry Dunnaway and their yellow lab, Ginger, Christie Swiger, Tim & Janet Bennett, Kenny & Tammy Daw and their sons Craig and Little Kenny, Dan & Jennifer Yerkes and occasionally others. We went almost every weekend.

Richard always was and still is "Mister Fix it." As we were sitting around our campfire one night, I noticed the lights dimming in my travel trailer. Richard told me that I needed to start my portable generator to charge up the trailer battery. We were camping without an electrical hookup. I started the generator and went back to sitting around the campfire. Soon, I noticed that the lights were dimmer than before. I asked Richard to walk over with me to help solve the problem and he readily agreed to go. When we got over there, Richard said, "You have to plug the trailer cord into the generator!" We returned to the campfire group, and all was well except for the ribbing from the group about my intelligence.

Enjoying the campfire was always on the evening agenda. Because of the size of our group, we circled almost entirely around the fire. Richard rode off on his scooter one night and when he returned, he was carrying a possum by the tail and dropped it right in the middle of our circle. The possum was excited upon its release but far less excited than the campfire group trying to get out of its way.

Richard always had most of the extra toys in the campground. He bought two jet skis and brought them along. He and I decided to go riding on them and take "the boys" (my twin sons, Alex and Andrew) to ride behind us. Andrew was with Richard and Alex was with me. After riding a few minutes, he decided that we would let the boys drive and we would sit behind them. Andrew only knows one speed and that is "wide open." He hit a big wave that threw Richard off the back, knocking the breath out of him. We still laugh to this day about that event.

Some nights, the younger people (not me) would play football and the football had a lighted plug in it. They didn't just play catch; they had opposing players trying to prevent you from catching it. As some might guess, the enthusiasm and play were excessive for nighttime play, and Christie's nose was broken in a collision. She was determined to be okay after a late-night hospital visit, but that ended nighttime football.

Richard decided to take Kelly and the boys riding in a wagon tied to his motor scooter. When they went through a ditch, the wagon turned over and all three kids fell in the mud. All the kids thought it was great fun and even their mothers were amused despite having to wash the mud from them.

Speaking of mud, Richard brought his John Deere Gator to the campground. The gator was a four-wheel drive, which meant that it had four wheels in the back and two wheels in the front. The water level of Lake Toho was very low which meant that much of the land previously underwater was available for riding. Richard and I decided to take Alex and Andrew for a ride that night at around 10 p.m., with them in the back bed of the gator and us in the front seat. Richard ventured too far out and the front-end of the gator dropped and sunk. We were stuck in the mud! Everyone still awake in the camp was needed to help. We finally decided to let the smallest kid, Andrew,

Our home away from home for trips and most weekends. Campsite #52 (Spring 2002)

drive so that all the adults and Alex could push. Andrew put the "pedal to the metal," throwing mud on all of us in the back. We finally got it out and had a lot of helpers to hose off! After showers in the campground showers, we were finally clean enough to enter our trailers and recover from our fun and exhaustion.

Our yellow Labrador, Simba, also enjoyed camping with us at Southport. He found his own friend and buddy in "Petey," the dog of campground owners Terry and Linda McGee. Petey was allowed to go into the campground store and Simba was allowed to go in with Petey. Other campers went into the store and played checkers for entertainment. After Simba had been in the lake swimming, he entered the store, walked over near the checker players, and decided to do the shake that dogs do to get water off them. Several adults were sprayed but all had become friends with the dogs and most thought it was funny.

Simba also loved to run, especially if he could run with Richard riding his scooter or the gator. Almost every evening Richard would take Simba for a run.

Simba would stay right with Richard, and they sometimes left the campground for their fun run. On one run with the gator, Simba found a skunk. Luckily, Simba stayed right with Richard and the gator, and they avoided a direct hit from the spray. It took all of us some time to determine that it wasn't a direct hit because the smell was so strong in the campground, and especially near Simba and the gator.

Usually, the weather was nice for camping, but we went camping regardless. Cold weather was seldom a problem, but we did have one trip that was near freezing weather with high winds. Determined to be outside, we hung sheets of plastic on wires connected between the trees to block the wind. That way, we could party, cook, and have our usual good time camping. Rain and thunderstorms were also a problem on a few occasions. Tim Bennett and I were on the lake fishing when the weather got horribly bad on the horizon toward the campground. We kept driving the boat further and further away from the campground to avoid the horrible weather, hoping that it would rain out before it got to us. Luckily for us, our plan worked. However, back at the campground, the weather was horrible with torrential rainfall and lightning. Everyone in the camp was extremely concerned about us! We were never in a drop of rain! When we got back to camp after the storm, Debi and Nita were pretty upset but finally calmed down after knowing that we were safe.

Another bad weather experience involved Richard, Dan Yerkes, and me when we had to come back to the campground through the horrible weather. We were in Richard's boat with a bimini top and one of the first fish finders with a GPS navigation system. The rain was coming down as hard as I have ever seen it rain. The sky was so dark that it looked like midnight. We could not see a foot in front of the boat. Dan and I held the bimini top down against the windshield and Richard slowly followed the GPS. We couldn't go very fast, nor could we see anything ahead of us. The GPS system worked perfectly, and by following it we finally arrived at the campground!

Southport Campground was our home away from home for several years, and we enjoyed it most weekends. The campground was finally closed after being purchased by someone else for airboat tours only. They took away our campground, but they cannot take away our memories of great fun and good times with our friends!

Kelly & the Boys

Camping with the Evans family so much resulted in a lot of times when Kelly, Alex, and Andrew were the only kids there to play together. Alex and Andrew were affectionately called "the boys" by most people. There was a four-and-a-half year age difference so when the boys were six, Kelly was one-and-a-half years old. Both boys enjoyed playing with her, and she would "squeal with delight" when they played with her. Debi, Kelly's mom, said that Kelly did not do that with any other kids that she played with—even those closer to her age.

When Kelly was two-and-a-half years old and the boys seven years old, she would hear some of the adults refer to Alex and Andrew as "the boys" and

Kelly (age 3) always corrected us. It's not "the boys" but "Kelly's boys." (July 2003)

Kelly would very emphatically say, “No, they are Kelly’s Boys!”

Richard made many power toys for Kelly. He made her a battery-powered Jeep. Kelly wasn’t too sure what to do with it, but Alex and Andrew were more than willing to drive it for her, and she quickly learned how much fun it was riding in the Jeep.

Though the age difference sometimes bothered the boys, they adored her as much as she did them. She was almost like a “little sister” to them part of the time, and they were careful to be protective of her. Richard’s latest toy for her was a jeep to ride made from an old lawnmower. He could set the speed and would set it much faster for the boys, but all the kids had fun driving it.

Sometimes it seemed that Richard was making toys for the boys as well as Kelly. I do know that there was certainly a lot of fun and excitement from enjoying the toys for Kelly and “the boys!” Great times for the kids...and the adults!

Camping at Townsend, Tennessee

We decided to make a camping trip with the Evans to Townsend, Tennessee. Those on the trip were Richard and Debi Evans with their daughter, Kelly and friend Janet Bennett, Nita and me, Alex, Andrew, and Simba.

We arrived close to Alex and Andrew's birthday and Debi had planned a special treasure hunt for them in the campground. After following the map all over the park, and in some cases having to dig up more clues, it all finally led back to the travel trailer of the Evans. The birthday present from the Evans was a money tree for each birthday boy with "money" for the leaves! They couldn't wait to take the leaves off, unroll the money to see how much loot they had gotten. It was a great birthday present and a great time following the map and finding everything that led to the gift!

Whitewater rafting was scheduled for the next day. Debi and Kelly took more of a floating trip since Kelly was too young for the whitewater trip. Richard, Janet, Nita, Alex, Andrew, and I took the whitewater trip.

How much fun can you have white water rafting...lots! (July 2003)

We were in a big rubber boat with a guide, and we went over some rocks and deep drop-offs. I almost fell out of the boat on one drop, much to the delight of the boys. We all made it safely to the bottom of the run after a great ride. It was one of the boys' favorite things that we did.

We also planned a biking trip around Cades Cove. I took Simba for a walk just before we planned to leave since we were planning to leave him in the trailer while we were all gone. While I was walking him on his leash, he pulled his head through the collar and was off. I couldn't get him to come back so I finally went back to the campground and got Nita and the boys to help me look for him. We told the Evans to go on to Cades Cove for the bike ride and we would join them after looking for Simba. We resumed the search with all of us thinking that we would never see Simba again. We finally found him in an adjacent campground making friends with the campers. Since he would run away from us just for fun, I assured a

The tough guy bikers are Cade's Cove ready for an 11-mile ride!

camper that he was friendly, and he agreed to hold Simba until I could walk up and put his collar and leash back on. We walked back to our trailer, put Simba inside, and headed to Cades Cove to join the Evans.

Cades Cove loop is an 11-mile, one-way road for bikers. The road goes up and down slight mountain hills and provides opportunities to see many kinds of wildlife. I had done the trip when I was much younger and decided to wait for everyone to return. Debi, Kelly, and Janet took a shorter version of the trip, but Richard, Nita, Alex, and Andrew did the full 11 miles. They saw deer and lots of wildlife, but Richard rode back part-way and was the only one to see a black bear.

Other activities on our trip included tubing in an ice-cold mountain stream, a day at Dollywood Amusement Park, a visit to underground caverns, horseback riding in the mountains, and hiking to a waterfall.

We all had a wonderful vacation with many exciting activities!

Surprise Trip to Texas

As a surprise for Nita's 25th birthday celebration, I decided to send her to visit her sister Debbie in Ft. Worth, Texas. When I say surprise, it was a total surprise up through the time that we left for the airport from work. We both were working at State Farm in Winter Haven, and I had made arrangements for her boss to let her off early to catch the plane and for a few days of vacation. She knew nothing! I had even decided to pack what she was taking in her suitcase. In my mind, I had packed all the essentials—clothes, makeup, underwear, etc. I had also bought her two birthday cards, one of which had her plane tickets enclosed. I had arranged for one of my employees to deliver the cards to Nita's desk while I waited out front with the car running for the dash to the airport. Everything was so exciting and working perfectly so far...

Her birthday is in October, and I had packed for her based-on Florida weather, which is nice in October. When she arrived in Dallas/Ft. Worth, the temperature was quite cold! Debbie was aware that she was coming. Unfortunately, I had not asked for her advice on packing, and I had not planned for the sudden weather change. Debbie was shocked to see the luggage, which was one teeny, tiny carry-on piece of luggage. I learned that a male's definition of the essentials was extremely lacking!

The good news for Nita was that she could wear a few of her sister's clothes but the great news was the opportunity and necessity for lots of shopping and new clothes.

It was certainly a memorable trip, is still discussed in the family, and far more costly than I had imagined!

Barn Building

In 1960, my dad decided to move our frame house from the lot it was on to another lot that he owned on Lake Parker. The total distance moved was probably a quarter mile. A few years later he decided to build a barn.

My dad was a person of great enthusiasm and determination, but frequently not real patient with the planning portion of projects. Using his three sons plus himself to do the labor, the task began.

The labor force and approximate ages of the workers were: James Owen Albritton (my dad), late 40s; James David, mid-20s; Edwin Arthur (me), early 20s; William Roy, (Bill) my younger brother, at about 10-12 years old. There was no one with any engineering knowledge of how to build a barn.

The plan was to build with used telephone poles that my dad had gotten for free. The first challenge after planning the layout of the barn was to figure out how we were going to get these long telephone poles to stand up without the proper equipment to raise them. My dad's idea and decision were to dig a hole with the post hole diggers and slant the top portion of the hole. We then built a rack on the back of the pickup truck in the shape of an X for the pole to lay in while we pushed it up vertically with the truck. We also had to put something else in the hole to keep the process from just pushing dirt and not standing up vertically.

You can imagine the work and determination involved in this process to get ONE pole vertical which was finally done successfully. I should mention that the barn had 9 bays requiring 16 poles and we finally had ONE upright. Two of the center bays were to have a second story which was to be the hay loft. The other one was left open to be high enough to hang the rope hoist for the butchering of beef.

After all the poles were upright, the next job was "notching" the posts so that the 2x8 or 2x10 lumber would rest on the pole notch when bolted to the post. We couldn't notch earlier since we probably would be unable to get each post planted at an exact depth.

The next step was framing it in and lastly, putting on a tin roof. We then installed a plywood floor for the hay loft.

I have no recollection of exactly how long this took, but I'm pretty sure it was weeks or months, not years or decades. Fortunately, all was done with no serious injuries or hospital trips, and the barn was useful for many years!

Built in the early 1960's for grove equipment, cattle feeding, and hay loft.

Dad Building Sunday School Attendance

My dad was asked to help build attendance up for the Young Adult Sunday School class at the Baptist church. He accepted and began visiting prospective members in their homes with my mom. The attendance immediately began increasing significantly. Some said that they had the easiest group to work with. After the numbers increased, making the class much larger, they moved on, and the numbers declined.

He did have trouble with one couple who seemed to enjoy the visits but never came to church. The visits continued without attendance. Finally, my dad asked why. The response was, "If we start attending, we are afraid that you will stop visiting us." They finally began attending.

Personal visitation was his secret but required more work than most were willing to do. This is one more example of how hard work and perseverance pays off.

Christi Early Reading

While in the waiting room at my dentist's office, I picked up the book *Hop on Pop* by Dr. Seuss, and was planning to read it to my daughter, Christi. As I opened the book, she began reading it out loud to me. She proceeded to read the entire book. I couldn't believe it! After the appointment was over, I immediately went to the bookstore, bought a copy, and recorded in the book that she read it at three-and-a-half years old! That was just the beginning.

The second experience happened when I was in the card shop looking for some cards. Christi would pick up cards and read them out loud to me. We began to draw a crowd of people coming over to watch the little kid reading all the cards. For some reason I thought that we should leave the card shop to protect her...from what I am not sure.

My third surprising experience was when Christi read the entire book, *Story Caravan*, at the age of four. The book has many stories, including a total of 1479 vocabulary words, and has a total of 279 pages. The book is the 3rd reader of the Sheldon Basic Reader series.

When reading out loud, Christi always used wonderful voice inflections in her reading. In the first grade, the teacher would read stories to the students. She finally decided to break the class into two groups and while she read to one of the groups, she would have Christi read to the other group. I wasn't sure if this was best for Christi, but I couldn't really see a problem big enough to interfere.

While she was so young and sitting on my lap to read, I suggested to her that if she would learn to read silently, she could probably read faster. She agreed to try this and we were each reading silently.

When she got to the bottom of the page and was ready to turn the page, she would ask if I had finished. I was not finished but would never admit that to her. I wanted her to read at her own pace. Obviously, reading the same book together came to an end.

This is the beginning of her wonderful experience with reading, and it continues.

Grand Canyon Cruise

Thanksgiving dinner at the Day household included several generations of families. Mamaw was the matriarch of the family and was there with her 3rd husband, Don. One of mom's "four" daughters, Jo, and her husband, Arty, had recently returned from a honeymoon cruise to the Grand Cayman Islands.

We were all talking about the cruise when Don (who has a hearing problem) said, "A cruise to the Grand Canyon, huh. I didn't know they had cruises there."

Loudly and in unison, we said, "Grand CAYMAN." He said, "Yes, I heard you, Grand Canyon. I didn't know that they had cruises there."

Everyone had their tickle box turned over by then, and I'm not sure how it ended other than with great laughter.

After Don and Mamaw left, we of course had a replay of the whole event. My brother-in-law, Greg, was more than willing to do the YMCA signaling with "Give me a C, give me an A, etc." for the replay. Great laughter within a great family event!

Family Shorts

Regarding marriage, my dad said: "You will marry someone that you date, so be careful!"

My grandfather said, "Love is just as likely to strike an outhouse as a mansion!"

Andrew asked his mom: "Do you know what A-S-S-H-O-L-E spells?"
She said, "Yes I do, asshole."

Andrew said, "Oh yeah, that's what you said when driving and someone pulled out on front of you."

Alex (when angry): "You're not my real Mommie! You look a lot like her but she's a lot nicer than you!!"

Alex & Andrew, age 10, found their mom's Master Christmas list with everything on it that they were getting! No surprises that year!

Emily, age 4 (niece): "Art's A Good Man."

Andrew: "Daddy, you're not the real boss, Mommie is!"

Dad: "You can have almost anything you want but you can't have everything you want."

Nita—Beloved Wife

No book, much less my life, would be complete without the story of Nita.

My life was in shambles in many ways after the divorce of my first marriage. Those details are best left untold. While attending a small church with my seven-year-old daughter, I noticed a beautiful young girl singing in the church choir. I was friends with the choir director, Lori, and her husband Jon. He wanted to introduce me to her. I agreed and after meeting Nita, it was obvious that we liked each other. When some of the church events were over, we began meeting to get something to eat. I had apple pie and coffee; she had French fries and diet coke. That was a hint to the next important piece of information in this story.

I was 38 years old at the time, and Nita was 19 years old. Obviously, that was a huge problem! While we couldn't care less what most people thought, nothing had been said to Nita's parents. Finally, she told them, and her father, Max, was very upset about it and did not want to meet me. He refused to even speak to me. Nita has three sisters, and they were quite upset too since the matter was upsetting the whole family. Nita was strong and insisted that she was going to continue seeing me. Her mom, Billie, finally agreed to meet me, which turned out to be most interesting.

After meeting her mom and exchanging pleasantries, I noticed a picture of the four daughters in evening dresses and said to her mom, "Three lovely daughters. You must be very proud." After a long delay, Nita finally said, "Three?" In my head, I could actually hear my voice saying three. How humiliating—and what a start to meeting her mother. Max continued mowing the yard.

We then began dating with me picking her up, going to dinner, movies or plays, and having a wonderful time. Max was always someplace else when I came over, and so the saga continued. I do remember thinking that I knew how he felt and would feel the same way—but I loved Nita! I do not remember exactly how that animosity ended, but I do know that Max ended up being very accepting of me and we had many wonderful years together. Back to my love of Nita.

Nita and I dated for three years. She was completing her degree at the University of South Florida in Tampa. I worked in Winter Haven at the State Farm Regional Office. One night each week, usually Wednesdays, we would meet halfway between Winter Haven and Tampa. I don't know the reason, but always at Burger King. Those meetings were so wonderful for each of us! For some reason, we never go to Burger King now.

Finally, I proposed to her. I bought the diamond ring and placed it in the trunk of a toy Mercedes convertible car and presented it to her as a gift. After encouraging her to open the trunk, she saw the ring and I asked her to marry me! She said "No!" We had previously discussed having children. I had decided before meeting Nita that I didn't plan to have any more children and had a vasectomy. Nita strongly wanted children and that was the deal breaker. The final decision was that she would marry me if we attempted to have children through a vasectomy reversal. That was a long journey. We married and the wedding and reception were some of the happy times. I would say happiest times but there were so many yet to come.

Nita began employment at State Farm's health department, and I continued my work in other departments. During these years, the vasectomy reversal was done with some success but resulting

Forty-one wonderful years and still counting... (January 11, 1998)

in no pregnancies. This continued for approximately seven years with tries and no positive results. Finally, we switched fertility specialist doctors from Tampa to Orlando. This was our final try, partly due to the cost, and partly due to the emotional drain. This time it was successful and not only was she pregnant, but pregnant with twins! Alex and Andrew were born! My daughter, Christi, was in college by now and almost grown. What a wonderful experience, having almost two completely different parenting experiences and children to love.

At this time, Nita and I have been married for 40 wonderful years and the love continues. Not one day goes by without me realizing that I am the luckiest man in the world! Nor does a day go by without telling each other and the kids "I love you." After all these years together, I am still amazed at her ability to love. She is the sweetest, most caring person that I have ever met. Somehow, I just got lucky and am still married to the most wonderful person in the world!

Jokes Introduction

For most of my life, I have enjoyed jokes and have saved many in paper form. My dad gave me a joke which he made a copy of on a Thermofax copy machine back in the 1950's. It's titled "Socialized Medicine—The Government Man." It is still one of my favorites and will be included in the collection for this book. It is still recirculated today, seventy years later. I have been saving that and many more since that time.

In 1989, I was asked to help emcee the afternoon session of an underwriting conference for a large insurance company for which I was employed. My first try at being an emcee! The morning session emcee did an effective job, and the last speaker of the morning was an actuary attorney who was so boring for an hour that it was the talk of the underwriters during lunch.

After lunch, I stepped up to the podium, commented about how much the number of attendees had grown, and said, "As Adam said to Eve: stand back we don't know how big this is going to get." The crowd, bored by the morning session, exploded in laughter! That memory helped inspire my interest in writing a book to share my favorite jokes.

One of my favorite categories of jokes relates to "communication" or the lack of it.

Another one of my favorite categories is sex-related jokes. My wife says of me, "He's still twelve years old." If I were around a situation today in which someone pulled off a surprise "whoopee cushion" sound on someone, I would fall apart laughing, thus proving once again that she is right.

A third category to me would be male vs female jokes and many of these are included. Both sides have their great moments in many.

Most important of all to me is that all categories create wonderful laughs and make life so much fun.

Knowing about my love of humor, people have been sharing jokes with me for years. “My cup runneth over” as well as my files. I haven’t read any joke books in many years. My experience with the ones that I did read back then was that you had to read the entire book to find a few good ones!

I hope that you find better luck when reading “my favorites!” While we all have a different sense of humor, I am confident that most of these will help brighten your day and put a smile on your face. Enjoy!

EAA

Favorite Jokes Index

Socialized Medicine—"The Government Man," 1971

The year is 1971. At this time, the American Government's policy of socialized medicine has been extended to require that any marriage that has not produced a child within the first five years of marriage must receive services of a government man who will attempt to be the means of the wife becoming a mother. There are no children in the family of this story, and it is the morning of their fifth anniversary.

The husband is preparing to leave for the office. He says, "Goodbye, dear. I suppose the Government man will be arriving shortly." He leaves with a bowed head. The wife makes herself pretty and powders her nose just as the doorbell rings. She opens the door, expecting the Government man. Instead, her caller is a baby photographer who has arrived in town with the hope that he can interest her in some baby pictures.

Lady: "Oh! Good morning."

Man: "How do you do? You don't know me, but I represent..."

Lady: "You needn't explain, Mr..."

Man: "Jones is the name, Madam, and I make a specialty of ..."

Lady: "Yes, I know—it's alright. Won't you come in?"

Man: "Your husband probably told you that..."

Lady: "Oh, yes, and we both agree that it is the only thing to do..."

Man: "Well, in that case, I may as well get busy."

Lady: "I'm not too familiar with the way you do this—just where do we start?"

Man: "Just leave that to me, madam. I recommend two in the bathtub, one or two more on the couch, and a couple on the floor."

Lady: "Bathtub? Floor? Good Heavens!"

Man: "Well, my dear lady! Even the best of us can't get a good one every time, but out of six, one is bound to be a honey. I usually have the best luck with the bathtub shot."

Lady: "You'll have to forgive me, but it does seem a little bit informal."

Man: "The charm of this whole thing is informality. Perhaps you'd like to see some of my work."

Lady: (blushing) "Well, I suppose—there's no hurry, is there?"

Man: "No, indeed! A man in my line of work can't do his best in a hurry. (He picks up the album and shows the baby pictures to her). Look at this baby, it's a good job. Took four hours, but isn't he a beauty?"

Lady: "Yes, indeed, a lovely child!"

Man: "But for a tough assignment, look at this job. Believe it or not, but this was done on top of a bus on Fifth Avenue."

Lady: "My Gosh!"

Man: "Well, there's a little story behind that. The mother of the child was a movie actress and needed a little publicity—and she got it!"

Lady: "I should think so...!"

Man: "Here is a picture of the handsomest twins in town. I knocked that one out in Central Park on a snowy afternoon last winter. It took me from two in the afternoon until five. I never worked under more difficult conditions, with people standing four and five rows deep trying to get a look."

Lady: "Four or five deep?"

Man: "Yes, people everywhere. Just imagine, more than three hours under a handicap like that. I even had two cops helping me. I could have gotten another quick shot or two before dark, but by that time, the squirrels were nibbling at my equipment, and I had to give up. Well, Madam, if you're ready, I'll set up my tripod and we'll get started."

Lady: "Your tripod?"

Man: "Yes, I always use a tripod to rest my equipment on as it's much too heavy to hold for any length of time and...Good Heavens. She fainted!"

Why Fishing Is Better Than Sex

#20 No matter how much whiskey you've had, you can still fish.

#19 A limp rod is still useful while fishing.

#18 You don't have to hide your fishing magazines.

#17 It is perfectly acceptable to pay a professional to fish with you once in a while.

#16 The Ten Commandments don't say anything against fishing.

#15 If your partner takes pictures or videotapes of you fishing, you don't have to worry about them showing up on the Internet if you become famous.

#14 Your fishing partner doesn't get upset about people you fished with many years ago.

#13 It's perfectly respectable to fish with a total stranger.

#12 When you see a really good fishing person, you don't have to feel guilty about imagining the two of you fishing together.

#11 If your regular fishing partner isn't available, he/she won't object if you fish with someone else.

#10 Nobody will ever tell you that you will go blind if you fish by yourself.

#9 When dealing with a fishing pro, you never have to wonder if they are really an undercover cop.

#8 You don't have to go to a sleazy shop in a seedy neighborhood to buy fishing stuff.

#7 You can have a fishing calendar on your wall at the office, tell fishing jokes, and invite coworkers to fish with you without getting sued for harassment.

#6 There are no fishing transmitted diseases.

#5 If you want to watch fishing on television, you don't have to subscribe to the Playboy channel.
#4 Nobody expects you to fish with the same partner for the rest of your life.
#3 Nobody expects you to give up fishing if your partner loses interest in it.
#2 You don't have to be a newlywed to plan a vacation primarily to enjoy your favorite activity.
#1 Your fishing partner will never say, "Not again? We just fished last week! Is fishing all you ever think about?"

Accident Details

Dear Sir:

I am writing in response to your request for additional information. In Block Number Three of the Accident Reporting Form, I put "trying to do the job alone" as the cause of my accident. You said in your letter that I should explain more fully, and I trust that the following details will be sufficient.

I am a bricklayer by trade. On the day of the accident, I was working alone on the roof of a new six-story building. When I completed my work, I discovered that I had about 500 pounds of brick left over. Rather than carry the bricks down by hand, I decided to lower them in a barrel by using a pulley, which was fortunately attached to the side of the building at the sixth floor.

Securing the rope at ground level, I went up to the roof, swung the barrel out, and loaded the brick into it. Then I went back to the ground, untied the rope, holding it tightly to ensure a slow descent of the 500 pounds of bricks. You will note in block number eleven of the accident reporting form that I weigh 135 pounds.

Due to my surprise at being jerked off the ground so suddenly, I lost my presence of mind and forgot to let go of the rope. Needless to say, I proceeded at a rather rapid rate up the side of the building.

In the vicinity of the third floor, I met the barrel coming down. This explains the fractured skull and broken collarbone.

Slowed only slightly, I continued my rapid ascent, not stopping until the fingers of my right hand were two knuckles deep into the pulley.

Fortunately, by this time I had regained my presence of mind and was able to hold tightly to the rope in spite of my pain.

At approximately the same time, however, the barrel of bricks hit the ground, and the bottom fell out of the barrel. Devoid of the weight of the bricks, the barrel now weighed approximately fifty pounds.

I refer you again to my weight of 135 pounds in block number eleven. As you might imagine, I began a rapid descent down the side of the building.

In the vicinity of the third floor, I met the barrel coming up. This accounts for the two fractured ankles and the lacerations of my legs and lower body.

The encounter with the barrel slowed me enough to lessen my injuries when I fell onto the pile of bricks and fortunately, only three vertebrae were cracked.

I am sorry to report, however, that as I lay there on the bricks, in pain, unable to stand, and watching the empty barrel six stories above me, I again lost my presence of mind: I let go of the rope.

Things That Sound Dirty but Aren't

At The Office
10. I need to whip it out by 5.
9. Mind if I use your laptop?
8. Just stick it in my box.
7. If I have to lick one more, I'll gag.
6. I want it on my desk, NOW!!!
5. Hmmmmmmmm...I think it's out of fluid!
4. My equipment is so old, it takes forever to finish.
3. It's an entry level position.
2. When do you think you will be getting off today?
And the number 1 thing that sounds dirty in the office but isn't:
1. It's not fair...I do all the work while he just sits there!

In Law
10. Have you looked through her briefs?
9. He is one hard judge!
8. Counselor, let's do it in chambers.
7. His attorney withdrew at the last minute.
6. Is it a penal offense?
5. Better leave the handcuffs on.
4. For $200 an hour, she better be good.
3. Can you get him to drop his suit?
2. The judge gave her the stiffest one he could.
And the number 1 thing that sounds dirty in law but isn't:
1. Think you can get me off?

At Thanksgiving
19. Talk about huge breasts!
18. Tying the legs together keeps the inside moist.

17. If I don't undo my pants, I'll burst!
16. Whew, that's one terrific spread!
15. Are you ready for seconds yet?
14. I'm in the mood for a little dark meat.
13. It's a little dry, do you still want to eat it?
12. It's Cool Whip time!
11. Do you think you'll be able to handle all these people at once?
10. You still have a little bit on your chin.
9. How long will it take after you stick it in?
8. You know it's ready when it pops up.
7. That's the biggest one I've ever seen!
6. Wow, I didn't think I could handle all of that!
5. How long do I beat it before it's ready?
4. I didn't expect everyone to come at once!
3. Don't play with your meat.
2. Just wait your turn, you'll get some!

And the number 1 thing that sounds dirty at Thanksgiving but isn't:

1. Just spread the legs open and stuff it in!

The Husband Store

A store that sells new husbands has opened in New York City where a woman may go to choose a husband. Among the instructions at the entrance is a description of how the store operates:

You may visit this store ONLY ONCE! There are six floors, and the value of the products increases as the shopper ascends stories. The shopper may choose any item from a particular floor or may choose to go up to the next floor, but you cannot go back down except to exit the building!

So, a woman goes to the Husband Store to find a husband. On the first floor the sign on the door reads:

Floor 1—These men Have Jobs.

She is intrigued, but continues to the second floor, where the sign reads:

Floor 2—These men Have Jobs and Love Kids.

'That's nice,' she thinks, 'but I want more.'

She continues upward. The third-floor sign reads:

Floor 3—These men Have Jobs, Love Kids, and are Extremely Good Looking.

'Wow,' she thinks, but feels compelled to keep going.

She goes to the fourth floor and the sign reads:

Floor 4—These men Have Jobs, Love Kids, are Drop-dead Good Looking and Help with Housework.

"Oh, mercy me!" she exclaims, "I can hardly stand it!"

Still, she goes to the fifth floor and the sign reads:

Floor 5—These men Have Jobs, Love Kids, are Drop-dead Gorgeous, Help with Housework, and Have a Strong Romantic Streak.

She is so tempted to stay, but she goes to the sixth floor, where the sign reads:

Floor 6—You are visitor 31,456,012 to this floor. There are no men on this floor. This floor exists solely as proof that women are impossible to please. Thank you for shopping at the Husband Store.

PLEASE NOTE:

To avoid gender bias charges, the store's owner opened a New Wives store just across the street.

The first floor has Wives that Love Sex.

The second floor has Wives that Love Sex and Money and Like Beer.

The third, fourth, fifth and sixth floors have never been visited.

Church Organist

Miss Beatrice, the church organist, was in her 80s and had never been married. She was admired for her sweetness and kindness to all. One afternoon, the pastor came to call on her and she showed him into her quaint sitting room. She invited him to have a seat while she prepared tea.

As he sat facing her old Hammond organ, the young minister noticed a cut-glass bowl sitting on top of it. The bowl was filled with water, and in the water floated, of all things, a condom! When she returned with tea and scones, they began to chat.

The pastor tried to stifle his curiosity about the bowl of water and its strange floater, but soon it got the best of him, and he could no longer resist. "Miss Beatrice", he said, "I wonder if you would tell me about this?" pointing to the bowl.

"Oh, yes," she replied, "Isn't it wonderful? I was walking through the park a few months ago and I found this little package on the ground. The directions said to place it on the organ, keep it wet and that it would prevent the spread of disease. Do you know, I haven't had the flu all winter."

The Purina Diet

I was in Wal-Mart buying a large bag of Purina for Harley and was in line to check out. A woman behind me asked if I had a dog........ Duh!

I was feeling a bit crabby, so on impulse, I told her no, I was starting The Purina Diet again, although I probably shouldn't because I'd ended up in the hospital last time, but that I'd lost 50 pounds before I was awakened in an intensive care unit with tubes coming out of most of my orifices and IVs in both arms. Her eyes about bugged out of her head.

I went on and on with the bogus diet story and she was totally buying it.

I told her that it was an easy, inexpensive diet and that the way it works is to load your pockets or purse with Purina nuggets and simply eat one or two every time you feel hungry. The package said the food is nutritionally complete so I was going to try it again.

I must mention here that practically everyone in the line was enthralled with my story by then, particularly the tall guy behind her.

Horrified, she asked if something in the dog food had poisoned me and whether that was why I ended up in the hospital.

I said, "No.....I'd been sitting in the street licking my butt when a car hit me."

I thought the tall guy was going to have to be carried out the door.

Are My Testicles Black?

A male patient is lying in bed in the hospital, wearing an oxygen mask over his mouth and nose, still heavily sedated from a difficult four-hour surgical procedure.

A young student nurse appears to give him a partial sponge bath.

"Nurse," he mumbles, from behind the mask, "Are my testicles black?"

Embarrassed, the young nurse replies, "I don't know sir, I'm only here to wash your upper body and feet."

He struggles to ask again, "Nurse, are my testicles black?"

Concerned that he may elevate his vitals from worry about his testicles, she overcomes her embarrassment and sheepishly pulls back the covers.

She raises his gown, holds his penis in one hand and his testicles in the other, lifting and moving them around. Then, she takes a close look and says,

"There's nothing wrong with them, Sir!!"

The man pulls off his oxygen mask, smiles at her and says very slowly, "Thank you very much. That was wonderful, but, listen very, very closely......

A r e - m y - t e s t - r e s u l t s - b a c k?"

President of Bank

A little old lady walked into the head branch of Chase Manhattan Bank holding a large paper bag in her hand. She told the young man at the window that she wished to take the $3 million she had in the bag and open an account with the bank.

She said that first though, she wished to meet the president of Chase Manhattan Bank due to the large amount of money involved. The teller seemed to think that was a reasonable request, and after opening the paper bag and seeing the bundles of $1,000 bills, which he was sure amounted to about $3 million, telephoned the bank president secretary to obtain an appointment for the lady.

The lady was escorted upstairs and ushered into the president's office. Introductions were made and she stated that she liked to get to know the people that she did business with on a more personal level. The bank president then asked her where she came into so much money. Did you inherit it? No, she replied.

He was quiet for a minute, trying to think of where this little old lady could have come into $3 million. I bet, she stated. You bet? repeated the bank president. As in horses? No, she replied. I bet people. Seeing his confusion, she explained that she just bets different things with people. Suddenly, she said, I'll bet you $25,000 that by 10:00 tomorrow morning your balls will be square.

The bank president figured that she must be off her rocker and decided to take her up on her bet. He didn't see how he could lose. For the rest of the day, the bank president was very careful. He decided to stay at home that evening and take no chances. There was $25,000 at stake.

When he got up in the morning and took his shower, he checked to make sure everything was okay. There was no difference. He looked the same as he always did. He went to the bank and waited for the little old lady to come in at 10:00. He knew this would be a good day. How often do you get handed $25,000 for doing nothing?

At ten o'clock sharp, the little old lady was shown into his office. With her was a younger man. When he inquired as to what his purpose for being there was, she informed him that the younger man was her lawyer, and she always took him along when there was that much money involved. Well, she asked him, what about our bet? I don't know how to tell you this but I'm the same as I've always been. Only $25,000 richer.

The lady seemed to accept this. But she requested that she be able to see for herself. The bank president thought this was reasonable and dropped his pants. She instructed him to bend over, and then grabbed his balls. Sure enough, everything was fine. The president then looked up and saw her lawyer standing across the room banging his head against the wall. What's wrong with him? he asked. Oh him, she replied. I bet him $100,000 that by 10:00 this morning, I'd have the president of Chase Manhattan Bank by the balls.

Ways to Annoy Your Public Bathroom Stall-mate

1. Stick your open palm under the stall wall and ask your neighbor, “May I borrow a highlighter?”
2. Say, “Uh oh, I knew I shouldn’t have put my lips on that.”
3. Cheer and loudly clap every time somebody breaks the silence with a bodily function noise.
4. Say, “Damn this water’s cold.”
5. Drop a marble and say, “Oh shit! My glass eye!”
6. Say, “Hmmm, I’ve never seen that color before.”
7. Drop a D-cup bra on the floor under the stall wall and sing “Born Free.”
8. Fill up a large flask with Mountain Dew. Squirt it erratically under your neighbor’s stall walls while yelling, “Whoa, Easy boy.”
9. Say, “Now how did that get in there?”
10. Say, “Interesting...more floaters than sinkers.”
11. Using a small squeeze tube, spread peanut butter on a wad of toilet paper and drop the wad under the wall of your neighbor. Then say, “Whoops, could you kick that back over here please?”
12. Say, “Hummus. Reminds me of hummus.”
13. Say, “C’mon Mr. Happy! Don’t fall asleep on me now.”
14. Fill a balloon with cream corn. Rush into the stall with your hand over your mouth and let out a lengthy vomit impression while you squeeze the balloon and splatter cream corn all about. Apologize profusely and blame it on the fettucine alfredo you had for breakfast.
15. Say, “Boy, that sure looks like a maggot.”
16. Say, “Damn, I knew that drain hole was a little too small. Now what am I gonna do.”

17. Play a well-known drum cadence repeatedly on your butt cheeks.
18. Before you unroll toilet paper, conspicuously lay down your "Cross-Dresser Anonymous" newsletter on the floor visible to the adjacent stall.
19. Grunt and strain real loud for 30 seconds and then drop a cantaloupe into the toilet bowl from a height of six feet. Sigh relaxingly.

Bored Casino Dealers

Two bored casino dealers were waiting at a craps table. A very attractive blond woman arrived and bet twenty thousand dollars on a single roll of the dice.

She said, "I hope you don't mind but I feel much luckier when I'm completely nude." With that, she stripped from her neck down, rolled the dice and yelled, "Mama needs new clothes!"

Then she hollered... "YES! YES! I WON! I WON!" She jumped up and down and hugged each of the dealers.

She then picked up all the money and clothes, and quickly departed.

The dealers just stared at each other dumbfoundedly. Finally, one of them asked, "What did she roll?" The other answered, "I don't know, I thought YOU were watching!"

Moral: Not all blondes are dumb, but all men are men.

Man, I'm Tired!

A man was sick and tired of going to work every day while his wife stayed home. He wanted her to see what he went through, so he prayed: "Dear Lord: I go to work every day and put in 8 hours while my wife merely stays at home. I want her to know what I go through, so please allow her body to switch with mine for a day. Amen." God, in his infinite wisdom, granted the man's wish.

The next morning, sure enough, the man awoke as a woman.

He arose, cooked breakfast for his mate, awakened the kids, set out their school clothes, fed them breakfast, packed their lunches, drove them to school, came home and picked up the dry cleaning, took it to the cleaners and stopped at the bank to make a deposit, went grocery shopping, then drove home to put away the groceries, paid the bills and balanced the check book. He cleaned the cat's litter box and bathed the dog. Then it was already 1 p.m., and he hurried to make the beds, do the laundry, vacuum, dust, and sweep and mop the kitchen floor. Ran to the school to pick up the kids and got into an argument with them on the way home. Set out milk and cookies and got the kids organized to do their homework, then set up the ironing board and watched TV while he did the ironing. At 4:30, he began peeling potatoes and washing vegetables for salad, breaded the pork chops, and snapped fresh beans for supper. After supper, he cleaned the kitchen, ran the dishwasher, folded laundry, bathed the kids, and put them to bed.

At 9 p.m., he was exhausted, and though his daily chores weren't finished, he went to bed where he was expected to make love, which he managed to get through without complaint.

The next morning, he awoke and immediately knelt by the bed and said: "Lord, I don't know what I was thinking. I was so wrong to envy my wife's being able to stay home all day. Please, oh! oh! please, let us trade back."

The Lord, in his infinite wisdom, replied: "My son, I feel you have learned your lesson, and I will be happy to change things back to the way they were. You'll just have to wait nine months though. You got pregnant last night."

Senior Pre-Nuptial Agreement

An elderly couple were about to be married.

She said: "I want to keep my house."
He said: "That's fine with me."

She said: "I want to keep my Cadillac."
He said: "That's fine with me."

She said: "I want to have sex six times a week."
He said: "Put me down for Fridays."

The Wedding Test

I was a very happy man. My wonderful girlfriend and I had been dating for over a year, and so we decided to get married. There was only one little thing bothering me... It was her beautiful younger sister.

My prospective sister-in-law was twenty-two, wore very tight miniskirts, and was generally bra-less. She would regularly bend down when she was near me, and I always got more than a nice view. It had to be deliberate. Because she never did it when she was near anyone else.

One day her "little" sister called and asked me to come over to check the wedding invitations. She was alone when I arrived, and she whispered to me that she had feelings and desires for me that she couldn't overcome. She told me that she wanted me just once before I got married and committed my life to her sister.

Well, I was in total shock, and couldn't say a word. She said, "I'm going upstairs to my bedroom, and if you want one last wild fling, just come up and get me."

I was stunned and frozen in shock as I watched her go up the stairs. I stood there for a moment, then turned and made a beeline straight to the front door. I opened the door and headed straight towards my car.

Lo and behold, my entire future family were standing outside, all clapping!

With tears in his eyes, my father-in-law hugged me and said, "We are very happy that you have passed our little test. We couldn't ask for a better man for our daughter. Welcome to the family."

And the moral of this story is: Always keep your condoms **in your car**!

Wrong Email Address

A Minneapolis couple decided to go to Florida to thaw out during a particularly icy winter. They planned to stay at the same hotel where they spent their honeymoon 20 years earlier. Because of hectic schedules, it was difficult to coordinate their travel schedules. So, the husband left Minnesota and flew to Florida on Thursday, and his wife flew down the following day.

The husband checked into the hotel. There was a computer in his room, so he decided to send an email to his wife. However, he accidentally left out one letter in her email address, and without realizing his error, sent the email.

Meanwhile, somewhere in Houston, a widow had just returned home from her husband's funeral. He was a minister who was called home to glory following a heart attack. The widow decided to check her email expecting messages from relatives and friends. After reading the first message, she screamed and fainted. The widow's son rushed into the room, found his mother on the floor, and saw the computer screen which read:

> To my loving wife. Subject: I've arrived. Date: October 16, 2005.
>
> "I know you're surprised to hear from me. They have computers here now and you are allowed to send emails to your loved ones. I've just arrived and have been checked in. I've seen that everything has been prepared for your arrival tomorrow. Looking forward to seeing you then!! Hope your journey is as uneventful as mine was.
>
> p.s. Sure is freaking hot down here!!!!"

Good Luck, Mr. Gorsky

On July 20, 1969, as commander of the Apollo 11 lunar module, Neil Armstrong was the first person to set foot on the moon. His first words after stepping on the moon, "That's one small step for man, one giant leap for mankind," were televised to earth and heard by millions.

But just before he reentered the lander, he made the enigmatic remark, "Good luck, Mr. Gorsky."

Many people at NASA thought it was a casual remark concerning some rival Soviet cosmonaut. However, upon checking, there was no Gorsky in either the Russian or American space programs. Over the years, many people questioned Armstrong as to what the "Good luck, Mr. Gorsky" statement meant, but Armstrong always just smiled.

On July 5, 1995, in Tampa, Florida, while answering questions following a speech, a reporter brought up the 26-year-old question to Armstrong.

This time he finally responded.

Mr. Gorsky had died, so Neil Armstrong felt he could answer the question. In 1938, when he was a kid in a small midwestern town, he was playing baseball with a friend in the backyard. His friend hit the ball, which landed in his neighbor's yard by the bedroom window. His neighbors were Mr. and Mrs. Gorsky. As he leaned down to pick up the ball, young Armstrong heard Mrs. Gorsky shouting at Mr. Gorsky. "Sex! You want sex?! You'll get sex when the kid next door walks on the moon!"

Drugstore Thermometer

This guy walked into the drugstore, and the druggist said, "Hi George, how are you?"

He said, "Don't say 'Hi George' to me, after what you said to my wife today over the telephone. I don't want anything to do with you anymore. We spend $100 a month in this place, and you had to talk like that to my wife."

The druggist said, "Now just a minute, just a minute! Let me tell you what happened to me this morning." He said, "I got up and there was 8 inches of snow on the ground." He said, "I went down, and I plugged in the coffee pot, and I went back up to shave and my wife had used my razor on her legs, and it was my last blade. It was so dull, I cut myself to pieces. I finally finished shaving and I came back down, and the coffee pot was broken. I fiddled around for half an hour trying to fix it and finally it was time to go to work. I ran out, got in the car, backed out and the left rear tire was flat. I changed the tire out in the snow, started to back up again and the spare was flat. I came back in and called a cab, and all the cabs were busy because of the snow. I had to walk to work and when I got there, ten people were waiting, all mad, and I'd forgotten my keys in the ignition of the car. I turned around and I walked home. I got home and my wife was mad at me because I didn't have breakfast with her. I walked back to the store, opened it up and started to wait on a woman in the front of the store and the phone rang in the back. I ran back to answer it, tripped over the magazine rack, picked up the phone...and there was nobody there. I came back to the front of the store and started waiting on the woman again and the phone rang for the second time. I ran to answer it, tripped over a bottle of Jergen lotion, and it broke all over the floor. I picked up the phone and there was nobody there. I came back up, started waiting on the woman for the third time, and the phone rang for the third time. I ran back, slipped in the Jergen lotion, fell, cut my hand, picked up the telephone and it was *your wife.*

And she said, 'How do I use that rectal thermometer you sold me yesterday?' (pause). What would you have told her...?"

Mood Ring

Dear Abby,

My husband is not happy with my mood swings. The other day he bought me a mood ring so he would be able to monitor my moods.

When I'm in a good mood, it turns green.

When I'm in a bad mood it leaves a big f@*#ing red mark on his forehead! Maybe next time he'll buy me a diamond.

Sincerely,
Bitchy Wife

Fishing Permission

Steve and his buddies were hanging out and planning an upcoming fishing trip. Unfortunately, he had to tell them that he couldn't go this time because his wife wouldn't let him. After a lot of teasing and name-calling, Steve headed home frustrated.

The following week when Steve's buddies arrived at the lake to set up camp, they were shocked to see Steve. He was already sitting at the campground with a cold beer, fishing rod in his hand and a campfire glowing.

"How did you talk your missus into letting you go, Steve?"

"I didn't have to," he replied. "Yesterday when I left work, I went home and slumped down in my chair with a beer to drown my sorrow because I couldn't go fishing. Then the ol' lady snuck up behind me and covered my eyes and said, 'surprise.' When I peeled her hands back, she was standing there in a beautiful see-through negligee and she said, 'Carry me into the bedroom, tie me to the bed and you can do whatever you want.' So here I am!"

A Mismatched Pair of Gloves

A young man wished to purchase a present for his sweetheart, and after careful consideration, he decided on a pair of gloves. Accompanied by his sweetheart's sister, he went to a department store and bought a pair of white gloves. The sister purchased a pair of panties for herself. During the wrapping, the items got mixed up. The sister got the gloves, and the sweetheart got the panties. Without checking the contents, he sealed the package and sent it to her with this note.

Dearest Darling,

This is a little gift to show you I have not forgotten your birthday. I chose these because I noticed that you are not in the habit of wearing any when we go out in the evening. If it had not been for your younger sister, I would have chosen the long ones with the buttons, but she wears the short ones that are very easy to remove. These are a delicate shade, but the lady I bought them from showed me a pair she had been wearing for three weeks and they were hardly soiled. I had the salesgirl try them on for me and she really looked smart. I wish I could put them on you for the first time. No doubt other men's hands will come in contact with them before I have a chance to see you again.

When you take them off, blow in them before putting them away as they will naturally be a little damp from wearing. Be sure to keep them on when you clean them, or they might shrink. I hope that you like them and will wear them for me on Friday night. All my love.

P.S. The latest style is to wear them folded down with the fur showing.

Ghosts

At a conference on the supernatural, one of the speakers asked, "Who here has ever seen a ghost?" Most of the hands go up. "And how many of you have had some form of interaction with a ghost?" About half of the hands go up. "Okay, now how many of you have had *physical* contact with a ghost?" Three hands stay up. There's a slight murmur in the crowd. "Gosh, that's pretty good. Okay, have any of you ever, uh...been intimate with a ghost?" One hand stays up. The speaker blinks. "Gosh, sir, are you telling us that you've actually had *sexual* contact with a ghost?"

The fellow suddenly blushes and says, "Oh, I'm sorry... I thought you said goats!"

25th Anniversary Party

A couple was celebrating their 25th wedding anniversary and a big party was given for the occasion. The man went off by himself and I found him looking up at the mountains. I asked him why he wasn't inside enjoying the festivities...25 years was quite an accomplishment!

He said, "Actually, after five years I wanted to kill her. I talked to my attorney and he convinced me that I would be convicted of murder and have to serve twenty years in jail.

"You know, I was just thinking...today I'd be a free man!"

The Washcloth

I was due later in the week for an appointment with my gynecologist. Early one morning I received a call from the doctor's office telling me that I had been rescheduled for early that morning at 9:30 a.m. I had only just packed everyone off to work and school, and it was already around 8:45 a.m. The trip to his office took about 35 minutes, so I didn't have any time to spare. As most women do, I like to take a little extra effort over hygiene when making such visits, but this time I wasn't going to be able to make the full effort. I rushed upstairs, threw off my dressing gown, wet the washcloth that was sitting next to the sink, and gave myself a quick wash in "that area" to make sure I was at least presentable. I threw the washcloth in the clothes basket, donned some clothes, hopped in the car and raced to my appointment. I was in the waiting room only a few minutes when I was called in.

Knowing the procedure, as I'm sure you do, after undressing and putting on the hospital gown, I hopped up on the table, looked over at the other side of the room and pretended I was in Paris or some other place a million miles away. I was a little surprised when the doctor said, "My, we have made extra effort this morning, haven't we?" But I didn't respond. When the appointment was over, I heaved a sigh of relief and went home. The rest of the day was normal: some shopping, cleaning, cooking, etc.

After school, while my six-year-old daughter was playing, she called out from the bathroom, "Mom, where's my washcloth?" I told her to get another one from the cupboard. She said, "No, I need the one that was here by the sink. It had all my glitter and sparkles in it."

Mathematics Professor

A professor of mathematics sent a fax to his wife. It read,

"Dear Wife.

You must realize that you are 54 years old, and I have certain needs which you are no longer able to satisfy. I am otherwise happy with you as a wife and I sincerely hope that you will not be hurt or offended to learn that by the time that you receive this letter, I will be at the Grand Hotel with my 18-year-old teaching assistant. I'll be home before midnight.

Your husband."

When he arrived at the hotel, there was a faxed letter waiting for him that read as follows:

"Dear Husband.

You, too, are 54 years old and by the time you receive this letter, I will be at the Breakwater Hotel with the 18-year-old pool boy. Being the brilliant mathematician that you are, you can easily appreciate the fact that 18 goes into 54 a lot more times than 54 goes into 18. Don't wait up."

Not the Brightest

Two shrimp short of a Gump.
Not the sharpest knife in the drawer.
A few clowns short of a circus.
A few fries short of a Happy Meal.
A few beers short of a six-pack.
Dumber than a box of rocks.
A few peas short of a casserole.
Doesn't have all his cornflakes in one box.
The wheel is spinning but the hamster's dead.
One fruit loop shy of a full bowl.
A few feathers short of a whole duck.
All foam, no beer.
The cheese slid off his cracker.
Warning. Objects in mirror are dumber than they appear.
Couldn't pour water out of a boot with instructions on the heel.
Chimney's clogged.
Elevator doesn't go all the way to the top floor.
Her sewing machine is out of thread.
His antenna doesn't pick up all the channels.
His belt doesn't go through all the loops.
Missing a few buttons on his remote control.
No grain in the silo.
Receiver is off the hook.
Skylight leaks a little.
Slinky's kinked.

Salesman of the Year

A young guy from Texas moves to California and goes to a big department store looking for a job.

The manager says, "Do you have any sales experience?"

The kid says, "Yeah, I was a salesman back home in Texas."

Well, the boss liked the kid, so he gave him the job. "You start tomorrow. I'll come down after we close and see how you did."

His first day on the job was rough, but he got through it. After the store was locked up, the boss came down. "How many sales did you make today?"

The kid says "one."

The boss says, "Just one? Our salespeople average 20 or 30 sales per day. How much was the sale for?"

The kid says, "$101,237.64."

The boss says "$101,237.64? What the hell did you sell?"

"First, I sold him a small fish hook. Then I sold him a medium fish hook. Then I sold him a larger fish hook. Then I sold him a new fishing rod. Then I asked him where he was going fishing, and he said down at the coast, so I told him he was gonna need a boat. We then went down to the boat department, and I sold him that twin engine Chris Craft. Then he said that he didn't think his Honda Civic would pull it. Then I took him down to the automotive department and sold him that 4x4 Blazer."

The boss said, "A guy comes in here to buy a fish hook and you sold him a boat and truck?"

"No, he came in here to buy a box of tampons for his wife, and I said, 'Well, your weekend's shot, you might as well go fishing!'"

Newspaper Ad

Newspaper Ad on Monday:

F.D. Brown has one sewing machine for sale. Phone 393-7409 after 6 p.m. and ask for Mrs. Smith who lives with him cheap.

Newspaper item on Tuesday:

Notice. We regret having erred in F.D. Brown's ad yesterday. It should read One sewing machine for sale. Cheap. Phone 393-7409 and ask for Mrs. Smith who lives with him after 6 p.m.

Newspaper item on Wednesday:

F.D. Brown has informed us that he has received several annoying phone calls because of the error we made in his classified ad yesterday. His ad stands corrected as follows: F.D. Brown has one sewing machine for sale. Cheap. Phone 393-7409 after 6 p.m. and ask for Mrs. Smith who loves with him.

Newspaper item on Thursday:

Notice! I, F.D. Brown, have no sewing machine for sale. I smashed it. The telephone has been taken out. I have not been carrying on with Mrs. Smith, my housekeeper. Yesterday she quit!

Make a List

A man says to his wife, "I want some ice cream."

She says, "Me too. Do you want me to write it down for you?"

"No," he says, "I can remember 'ice cream.'"

"Well, while you are there, why don't you get us some chocolate syrup?"

He says, "Good idea."

His wife says, "Do you want me to write it down for you?"

"No, I can remember ice cream and chocolate syrup."

Just as he is about to leave, she says, "I think we should get some nuts to go on it."

He says, "Okay, sounds good."

"Do you want me to write it down for you?"

"No, I can remember ice cream, chocolate syrup and nuts."

He's gone for about twenty minutes, comes in and puts the package down. She opens it and it's a dozen eggs! She looks at it and says, "You should have let me write it down for you. You dummy, you forgot the bacon!"

Shorts

Doe Leaving Woods—Do you know what the doe said when she came out of the woods? "That is the last time I'll do that for two bucks."

Get on the Ball—A minister went out to play golf. He teed the ball up on an ant hill. After a few swings missed the ball completely, he had killed all the ants but two. One ant looks at the other and says, "If we are going to get out of this mess alive, I think we'd better get on the ball!"

Miss you—A couple is lying in bed. The man says, "I am going to make you the happiest woman in the world." The woman says, "I'll miss you."

Success—A man says, "Since I first laid eyes on you, I've wanted to make love to you really badly." She says, "Well, you succeeded."

Switch—He says, "Shall we try swapping positions tonight?" She says, "That's a good idea. You stand by the ironing board while I sit on the sofa and fart."

Grocery $—He says, "What have you been doing with all the grocery money I gave you?" She says, "Turn sideways and look in the mirror."

Question—What do you call an intelligent, good looking, sensitive man? A rumor.

Marriage—Someone defines bigamy as having one spouse too many and monogamy as being the same thing.

Youth—You are only young once, but it makes you tired for the rest of your life.

Office—Do you know what it means to go to an office where your opinion is appreciated and your supervisor treats you as an equal? It means you've gone to the wrong office!

Fishing—Two men were fishing on Sunday. At about 11:00 a.m., one says, "My preacher is just stepping into the pulpit. I should be there." The other fisherman says, "I couldn't go even if I were home, my wife's sick."

Architect—A man returns to the small agricultural area where he grew up and decided to build a house. After presenting his house plans to the local builder for review, he gets a call asking, "Mr. Smith, who drew up these house plans for you?" The man responds that they were done by an architect. He replied, "Well, I can build it this way, but the bathroom will be on the inside!" (Things do change, now we cook outside.)

Wisdom—At a local political rally in the park, the speaker says, "The main problems of this country are ignorance and apathy." Two drunks in the park overhear this. One drunk says to the other, "What does that mean?" The other one says, "I don't know, and I don't give a damn!"

Sex and Snow—What does sex and snow have in common? You never know how long it will last or how many inches you'll get.

Confidence—A presidential candidate at an election was so confident on election night that he said to his wife, "Darling, tomorrow night you are going to sleep with the President of the United States." How's that for confidence? Well, the next night after the vote was counted, she said, "How do we work this out, do I go over there, or does he come over here?"

Longevity—Married men live longer than single men, but married men are a lot more willing to die.

Discussion Technique—A woman has the last word in any argument. Anything a man says after that is the beginning of a new argument.

Bugging You—Old aunts used to come up to me at weddings, poking me in the ribs and telling me, "You're next." They stopped after I started doing the same thing to them at funerals.

Bathroom Break—If you gotta go, you've gotta go. If you don't go when you gotta go, you find out that you've done been.

Marriage—A woman marries a man expecting he will change but he doesn't. A man marries a woman expecting that she won't change but she does.

Dressing Up—A woman will dress up to go shopping, water the plants, empty the trash, answer the phone, read a book, and get the mail. A man will dress up for weddings and funerals.

Natural—Men wake up as good-looking as they went to bed. Women somehow deteriorate during the night.

Offspring—Ah, children. A woman knows all about her children. She knows about dentist appointments and romances, best friends, favorite foods, secret fears and hopes and dreams. A man is vaguely aware of some short people living in the house.

Mistakes—A married man should forget his mistakes. There's no use in two people remembering the same thing.

Friendship—A woman didn't come home one night. The next morning, she told her husband that she had slept over at a friend's house. The man called his wife's 10 best friends. None of them knew anything about it. A man didn't come home one night. The next morning, he told his wife that he had slept over at a friend's house. The woman called her husband's 10 best friends. Eight confirmed that he had slept over, and two said that he was still there.

Nicknames—If Laura, Kate, and Sarah go out for lunch, they will call each other Laura, Kate, and Sarah. If Mike, Dave, and John go out, they will affectionately refer to each other as Fat Boy, Godzilla, and Four-eyes.

Bathrooms—A man has six items in his bathroom: a toothbrush and toothpaste, shaving cream, a razor, a bar of soap, and a towel. The average number of items in a typical woman's bathroom is 337. A man would not be able to identify more than 20 of these items.

Eating Out—When the bill arrives, Mike, Dave, and John will each throw in $20 even though it's only for $32.50. None of them will have anything smaller and none will actually admit they want change back. When the girls get their bill, out come the pocket calculators.

Money—A man will pay $2 for a $1 item he needs. A woman will pay $1 for a $2 item that she doesn't need but is on sale.

Future—A woman worries about the future until she gets a husband. A man never worries about the future until he gets a wife.

Success—A successful man is one who makes more money than his wife can spend.

45—What's the difference between a girlfriend and a wife? 45 lbs. What's the difference between a boyfriend and a husband? 45 minutes.

Journey—One sperm says to the other, "How far is it to the ovaries?" The other one says, "Relax. We just passed the tonsils."

Cost—What is it when a man talks nasty to a woman? Sexual harassment. What is it when a woman talks nasty to a man? $3.99 per minute.

Sex—What is the definition of "making love?" Something a woman does while a guy is f@*#ing her.

Size—A midget sidles up to a tall blonde and says, "Hey, what do you say to a little f@*#?" She says, "Hello, you little f@*#."

Paint—Did you hear about the new blonde paint? It's not real bright, but it's cheap and spreads easy.

Dead—How can you tell if your wife is dead? The sex is the same, but the dishes pile up. How can you tell if your husband is dead? The sex is the same, but you get the remote.

Identification—The young lady stood at the teller's desk in the bank. The teller looked at the check she wished to cash and asked her if she could identify herself. For a moment she seemed bewildered. Then she pulled a small mirror from her handbag, glanced in it, and said, "Yes. This is me alright."

Dead Cat—A kindergarten pupil told his teacher he'd found a cat. She asked him if it was dead or alive. "Dead," she was informed. "How do you know?" she asked her pupil. "Because I pissed in its ear and it didn't move," answered the child innocently. "You did *what*?" the teacher exclaimed in surprise. "You know," explained the boy, "I leaned over and went 'Pssst!' and it didn't move."

Open microphone—It was that time during the Sunday morning service: the children's sermon. All the children were invited to come forward. One little girl was wearing a particularly pretty dress and as she sat down, the pastor leaned over and said, "That is a very pretty dress. Is it your Easter dress?" The little girl replied directly into the pastor's clip-on microphone. "Yes, and Mom says that it's a bitch to iron."

Arithmetic—Little Johnny returns from school and says that he was expelled due to math class. "Why?" asks the father. "The teacher asked, 'How much is 2x3?' and I said '6.'"

"But, that's right!"

"Then she asked me, 'What is 3x2?'"

"What's the f@*#ing difference?" asks the father.

"That's what I said!"

Riddle—What does Arnold Schwarzenegger have that's real long, Kevin Costner have that's fairly long, Madonna doesn't have, the Pope have but doesn't use?

..........last name!!!! What were you thinking?

Warm hand—A speaker had received a deafening roar of applause following his introduction. Looking out over the audience, he said, "As the cow said to the farmer on a winter day, thanks for the warm hand!"

Homework—A little boy was doing his math homework. He said to himself, "Two plus five, that son of a bitch is seven. Three plus six, that son of a bitch is nine..." His mother heard what he was saying and gasped, "What are you doing?" The little boy answered, "I'm doing my math homework, Mom." And this is how your teacher taught you to do it?" the mother asked. "Yes," he answered. Infuriated, the mother asked the teacher the next day, "What are you teaching my son in math?" The teacher replied, "Right now, we are learning addition." The mother asked, "And you are teaching them to say two plus two, that son of a bitch is four?" After the teacher stopped laughing, she answered, "What I taught them was, two plus two, the sum of which is four!"

Census—A woman working as a census worker walked up to a mountaineer sitting on his porch. In trying to explain why she was there, she said to the man, "I work for the U.S. Government Census Bureau, and we are trying to find out how many people there are in America." He said, "Well, I ain't got the faintest idea!"

Blacksmith—A blacksmith hired a new apprentice kid, just out of high school, back when they used to shoe horses. They were going to shoe their first horse. He got the kid in there to teach him what to do. The blacksmith picked up the shoe with the tongs, stuck it in the fire, got it good and hot. He handed the kid a sledgehammer and said, "Now when I nod my head twice, hit it as hard as you can with the hammer...(pause)." Pity, he left a widow and two children. The guy's six feet under the sod because he didn't know how to communicate effectively. How can we get our ideas across to other people clearly?

Stuck-Up—The kid opened the door to let the neighbor lady in. "I heard my father say you were stuck-up," he greeted her. "How much did they get?"

Church Sign—I saw a sign on a church marquee that said, "What Is Hell Like? Come hear our new minister."

My Children—A very macho Italian man had three sons, all dark-skinned much like him, and he was very proud of them. His wife was Swedish, and their fourth son was very fair-skinned. The wife was dying on her deathbed. He said to her, "I know we only have a few minutes left together, but I gotta know...our fourth son, is he mine?" She said, "Yes, but the other three aren't!" Then she died...with a big smile on her face.

Shopper Dad—Customers in a busy supermarket couldn't help but notice a man pushing a cart with a screaming baby. The father shouted repeatedly: "Don't get excited, Albert. Don't scream, Albert. Don't yell, Albert. Keep calm, Albert." A woman finally stepped forward and said, "You certainly are to be commended for trying to soothe your son."

"He's Donald, I'm Albert," the father solemnly informed her.

Fashionable Hotel Sign—After paying her bill at the fashionable hotel, the lady noticed a sign that read: "Have you left anything?" It prompted her to go back and speak to the manager. "That sign is wrong," she said. It should read: "Have you anything left?"

Judgement—Husband: "You must admit it, men have better judgment than women." Wife: "Oh, yes, I agree. You married me and I married you."

Dentist Visit—The husband and wife entered the dentist's office.

"I want a tooth pulled," the wife said. "I don't want gas or injections, since I am in a terrible hurry. Just pull out the tooth as quickly as possible."

"You certainly are a brave woman," said the dentist. "Now show me which tooth it is."

She turned to husband: "Open your mouth, Bill."

Language—A man was traveling and while in a restaurant, he asked the waitress, "How far to San Josey?"

She said, "Here J is pronounced as H, so it's San Jose. How long are you going to be in San Jose?"

He said, "I don't know, probably until Hune or Huly."

Age—A tourist spotted an old-timer sitting on his porch in a rocking chair. "Have you lived here all your life?" asked the tourist.

"Not yet," the old man replied.

New Hire—A young man who had been hired by the personnel department of a large supermarket chain reported to work at one of the stores. The manager greeted him with a warm handshake, handed him a broom, and said, "Your first job will be to sweep out the store."

"But," said the young man, a bit deflated, "I'm a college graduate."

"I'm sorry," said the manager, "I didn't know that. Here, give me the broom and I'll show you how."

Disagreement—Two salesmen who were driving in Massachusetts and headed for the city of Peabody disagreed on the correct pronunciation. One said it was Peabody and the other Peabody. Upon arrival, they stopped to eat, and agreed to let the waitress decide the issue. One man asked her, "Would you please pronounce the name of the place we are in very slowly?"

"Sure," she replied, "it's BUR...GER...KING!"

Censorship—During a censorship survey, an elderly woman was asked if she thought there was too much sex and violence in cinemas today. "Can't really say," she answered. "I always sit in the front row in order to see and hear better, and I never notice what the rest of the audience is doing."

Kid Humor—One of my seven-year-old twin boys provided the following joke material twenty-three years ago. "Why did Tigger stick his head in the toilet?" Answer: "To look for Pooh!"

Belief is All You Need

A man was lost while driving through the country. As he tried to read a map, he accidently drove off the road into a ditch. Though he wasn't injured, his car was stuck deep in the mud. So the man walked to a nearby farm to ask for help.

"Warwick can get you out of that ditch," said the farmer, pointing to an old mule standing in a field. The man looked at the haggard mule, and looked at the farmer who just stood there repeating, "Yep, old Warwick can do the job." The man figured he had nothing to lose. The two men and Warwick made their way back to the ditch.

The farmer hitched the mule to the car. With a snap of the reins he shouted, "Pull Fred! Pull Jack! Pull Ted! Pull Warwick!" And the mule pulled the car from the ditch with very little effort.

The man was amazed. He thanked the farmer, patted the mule and asked, "Why did you call out all of those other names before you called Warwick?

The farmer grinned and said, "Old Warrick is just about blind. As long as he believes he's part of a team, he doesn't mind pulling."

Living Life Backwards

The most unfair thing about life is the way it ends. I mean, life is tough. It takes up a lot of your time. And, then you die. What's that? A bonus? I think the life cycle is all backwards.

You should die first and get it all over with.
Then you live in an old age home.
You get kicked out when you're too young.
You get a gold watch.
You go to work.
You work forty years until you're young enough to enjoy retirement.
You get ready for high school, drink alcohol, party and be promiscuous.
You go to grade school and become a kid.
You play. You have no responsibilities.
You become a little baby and go back into the womb.
You spend your last nine months floating.
Then, you finish off as an orgasm!

Variations of this piece have also been misattributed to Andy Rooney, George Carlin and Woody Allen. The original source is a variation on a piece by Sean Morey.

Little Johnny

Multi-syllable words—The teacher says to the class, "Today we are going to learn multi-syllable words. Does anybody have an example of a multi-syllable word?" Johnny raises his hand and says, "Me, Miss Rogers, I do." Miss Rogers says, "Alright, Johnny what is your multi-syllable word? Johnny says, "Mas-turbate." Miss Rogers smiles and says, "Wow, Johnny that's a mouthful." Johnny says, "No, Miss Rogers, you're thinking of a blowjob."

Correct word—Little Johnny was sitting in class one day when all of a sudden, he needed to go to the bathroom. He yelled out, "Miss Jones, I need to take a piss." The teacher replied, "Now, Johnny, that is not the proper word to use in this situation. The correct word is urinate. Please use the word urinate in a sentence correctly, and I will allow you to go." Johnny thinks for a bit, then says, "You're an eight but if you had bigger tits, you'd be a ten!"

Beautiful—One day during a lesson on proper grammar, the teacher asked for a show of hands from those who could use the word "beautiful" in the same sentence twice. First, she called on Suzie who responded with, "My father bought my mother a beautiful dress and she looked beautiful in it."

"Very good, Suzie," replied the teacher. She then called on Michael. "My mommy planned a beautiful banquet and it turned out beautifully," he said. "Excellent, Michael." Then the teacher called on Johnny. He said, "Last night at the dinner table, my sister told my father that she was pregnant and he said, 'Beautiful...just f@*#ing beautiful!'"

Saying the Right Thing

Jack wakes up at home with a huge hangover after the night of his office Christmas party. He forces himself to open his eyes, and the first thing he sees is a couple of aspirins next to a glass of water on the side table. And, next to them, a single red rose!

Jack sits down and sees his clothing in front of him, all clean and pressed. Jack looks around the room and sees that it is in perfect order, spotlessly clean. So is the rest of the house. He takes the aspirins, cringes when he sees a huge black eye staring back at him in the bathroom mirror, and notices a note on the table, "Breakfast is on the stove, I left early to go shopping—Love you."

He stumbles to the kitchen and sure enough, there is hot breakfast and the morning newspaper. His son is also at the table eating. Jack asks, "Son...what happened last night?"

Jack's son answers, "Well, you came home after 3 a.m., drunk and out of your mind. You broke some furniture, puked in the hallway, and got that black eye when you ran into the door!"

Jack says, "So, why is everything in such perfect order, so clean, I have a red rose, and breakfast is on the table waiting for me?"

His son replies, "Mom dragged you to the bedroom, and when she tried to take your pants off, you screamed, 'Leave me alone, lady, I'm married!'"

Broken furniture - \$85.26
Hot Breakfast - \$4.20
Red Rose bud -\$3.00
Two Aspirins -\$0.38

Saying the right thing, at the right time . . . **Priceless!!**

Assassin Interview Test

The CIA had an opening for an assassin. After all of the background checks, interviews, and testing were done, there were three finalists: two men and a woman.

For the final test, the CIA agents took one of the men to a large metal door and handed him a gun. "We must know that you will follow your instructions, no matter what the circumstances are. Inside this room, you will find your wife sitting in a chair. Kill her."

The man said, "You can't be serious. I could never shoot my wife."

The agent said, "Then you are not the right man for this job."

The second man was given the same instructions. He took the gun and went into the room. All was quiet for about five minutes. Then the man came out with tears in his eyes. "I tried, but I can't kill my wife."

The agent said, "You don't have what it takes. Take your wife and go home."

Finally, it was the woman's turn. She was given the same instructions to kill her husband. She took the gun and went into the room. Shots were heard, one after another. They heard screaming, crashing, banging on the walls. After a few minutes, all was quiet.

The door opened slowly and there stood the woman. She wiped the sweat from her brow and said, "This gun is loaded with blanks! I had to beat him to death with the chair!"

Ice Fishing

Two experienced fishermen went ice fishing. They chopped holes in the ice about 25 feet apart, put worms on their hooks, dropped their lines in the water, and got nary a nibble. This went on for several hours, but no luck. Midafternoon, a schoolboy arrived, walked confidently onto the ice, chopped his hole between those of the two men, and caught fish after fish.

The men were amazed, and finally one approached the boy and asked, "Tell me, young man, what's your secret?"

The boy replied, "Mmmm yymmm mmms wmmm."

"What's that?" asked the man. "Say it again, please."

The boy said, "Mmmm yymmm mmms wmmm."

The man repeated, "I'm sorry. I just can't understand you. Would you speak a little more clearly?"

At that, the boy cupped his palms, spat a large amount of substance into them, and said clearly, "Keep your worms warm."

(It's not only what you know, but are you willing to *do* it?)

Antique Dealer

There was an antique dealer who was shopping around several rural junk shops when he spotted a cat sipping milk out of a very valuable bowl.

He wanted to buy that bowl, but he didn't want the junk shop owner to know just how valuable it was. He decided to trick him into selling him the bowl.

He said to the owner, "That's a very cute little cat you've got there."

The owner just said, "Yep."

The dealer said, "My granddaughter used to own a cat that looked just like that, but it ran away."

The owner just nodded.

The dealer said, "I'd give anything to surprise her by bringing a cat like that home. Would you consider selling that cat?"

The owner said, "Might."

The dealer said, "I'll give you fifty bucks cash."

The owner said, "Sold."

They exchanged the money and the antique dealer said, "You know, the cat seems pretty attached to that bowl. You don't mind if I take that along too, do you?"

The owner said, "Oh, I couldn't let you have that. That's my lucky bowl. You wouldn't believe it, but since I've been putting the milk in that bowl, I've sold fifteen of them fifty-dollar cats."

Retirement Fun

I frequently ask retired people what they do to make their days interesting. This is what one guy told me.

I went to the store the other day, parked my car, and was on the way in when a youngster parked his car, jumped out, pushed me aside and snapped, "Move, old-timer, I'm in a hurry."

Well, I was in there for only about five minutes. When I came out, there was a cop writing out a parking ticket.

I went up to him and said, "Come on buddy, how about giving a senior a break?" He ignored me and continued writing the ticket. I called him a Nazi. He glared at me and starting writing another ticket for having worn tires. So, I called him a piece of dog sh*t. He finished the second ticket and put it on the windshield with the first. Then he started writing a third ticket. This went on for about twenty minutes. The more I abused him, the more tickets he wrote.

Personally, I didn't give a damn. My car was parked around the corner. He was ticketing the car of that smart ass youngster.

I try to have a little fun each day now that I am retired. It's important at my age!

Genie Bottle

A guy goes into a bar, sits on a stool, reaches into his pocket, and sets a little piano on the bar. He reaches into his other pocket and takes out a little man and sets it on the bar. The little man starts playing the piano like crazy.

The man beside him at the bar says, "What's going on?"

"Well, I found this little bottle, rubbed it, and a genie appeared and said, 'I grant you one wish.'"

"Do you think it would work for me?"

"I don't know. Here, try it."

He rubs the bottle, then a genie appears and says, "I'll grant you one wish."

The guy says, "I want a million bucks."

The place starts filling up with ducks...ducks everywhere!

He says, "What's happening?"

The first guy says, "I don't know. You don't think I asked for a 12-inch pianist, do you?"

The Whole Story

Little Bobby watched his Daddy's car pass by the school playground and go into the woods. Curious, he followed the car and saw Daddy and Aunt Jane in a passionate embrace.

Little Bobby found this so exciting that he could not contain himself as he ran home and started to tell his mother.

"Mommy, I was at the playground and I saw Daddy's car go into the woods with Aunt Jane. I went back to look and he was giving Aunt Jane a big kiss. Then, he helped her take off her shirt. Then Aunt Jane helped Daddy take his pants off. Then Aunt Jane..."

At this point, Mommy cut him off and said, "Bobby, this is such an interesting story, suppose you save the rest of it for suppertime. I want to see the look on Daddy's face when you tell it tonight."

After dinner, Mommy asked Bobby to tell his story. Bobby started his story about the car going into the woods, the undressing, Aunt Jane laying down on the backseat. Then, Aunt Jane and Daddy started doing the same thing that Mommy and Uncle Bill used to do when Daddy was in the Army!

Moral of the story—Sometimes you need to listen to the <u>whole</u> story before you interrupt.

New Radio

Someone who teaches at a middle school in Hudson, Florida forwarded the following letter. The letter was sent to the principal's office after the school had sponsored a luncheon for the elderly.

Dear Hudson Middle School:

God bless you for the beautiful radio I won at your recent senior citizens' luncheon. I am 84 years old and live at the Hudson Assisted Home for the aged. All of my family has passed away. I am all alone now, and it's nice to know that someone is thinking of me. God bless you for your kindness to an old forgotten lady.

My roommate is 95 and always had her own radio, but before I received one, she would never let me listen to hers, even when she was napping. The other day her radio fell off the nightstand and broke into several pieces.

It was awful and she was in tears. She asked if she could listen to mine, and I said, "F@*# you."

Life is good.

Sincerely,
Edna.

Bedroom Football

An old man and his wife had gone to bed. After laying there a few minutes, the old man farts and says, “Seven points.”

His wife rolls over and says, “What in the world was that?”

The old man replies, “It’s fart football.” A few minutes later the wife lets one go and says, “Touchdown, tie score.” After about five minutes, the old man farts again and says, “Touchdown, I’m ahead 14 to 7.

Not to be outdone, the wife rips another one and says, “Touchdown, tie score.” Five seconds go by and she lets out a squeaker and says, “Field goal. I lead 17 to 14.”

Now the pressure’s on and the old man refuses to get beat by a woman. He strains real hard but to no avail. Realizing a defeat is totally unacceptable, he gives it everything he has but instead of farting, he poops in the bed.

The wife looks and says, “What the hell was that?”

The old man replied, “Half-time, Switch sides!”

Donkey Racing in Texas

A preacher wanted to raise money for his church, and being told that there was a fortune in horse racing, he decided to purchase a horse and enter him in the races. However, at the local auction, the going price for horses was so steep that the preacher ended up buying a donkey. He figured that since he had it, he might as well go ahead and enter it in the races. The donkey came in third.

The next day, the daily racing form carried this headline:

"Preacher's ass shows."

The preacher was so pleased with the donkey that he entered it in the race again. This time it won! The form read:

"Preacher's ass out in front."

The bishops were so upset with this kind of publicity that they ordered the preacher not to enter the donkey in another race. The newspaper headline read:

"Bishop scratches preacher's ass."

This was too much for the bishop, and he ordered the preacher to get rid of the animal. The preacher decided to give it to a nearby convent. The headline the next day read:

"Nun has best ass in town."

The bishop fainted. He then informed the nun that she would have to dispose of the donkey. She finally found a farmer who was willing to buy the animal for $10. The next day the paper read:

"Nun peddles ass for ten bucks."

They buried the bishop the next day. The next day the headlines read:

"Too much ass responsible for bishop's death!"

Donnie and David

This woman raised a pair of these kids. She raised them on the theory of, you know, don't spank them, it might disturb their personality. Don't disagree with them, it might upset their psyche. Twin boys, Donnie and David. Well, they got to be 19 and she couldn't do anything with them. They were great big strapping teenagers, and finally in desperation, she went to the doctor and said, "Doctor, what am I going to do with Donnie and David?"

He was a doctor from the old school and said, "Do what you should have done 10 years ago. The next time one of them mouths off or swears, belt him one. But don't get mad."

She said, "I'll try it."

The next morning, they were sitting there at breakfast with glum looks on their faces, and she said, "Donnie, what would you like for breakfast?"

He said, "I'll have some of them damn cornflakes."

Boom, she hit him, and back against the wall he went, eyes wide, blood running out the side of his mouth. Very calmly, she turned to the other one and said, "David...what would you like for breakfast?"

He said, "I don't know, but I sure as hell don't want any of those damn cornflakes..."

Baked Beans

Once upon a time, there lived a man who had a maddening passion for baked beans. He loved them, but they always had a very embarrassing and somewhat lively reaction on him. Then one day he met a girl and fell in love. When it was apparent that they would marry, he thought to himself, "She is such a sweet and gentle girl, and she will never go for this kind of carrying on." So, he made the supreme sacrifice and gave up baked beans. They were married shortly thereafter.

Some months later, his car broke down on the way home from work. Since they lived in the country, he called his wife and told her that he would be late as he had to walk home. On his way, he passed a small café and the odor of freshly baked beans was overwhelming. Since he still had several miles to walk, he figured that he would work off any ill effects before he got home. So he stopped at the café. Before he left, he had eaten three large orders of baked beans. All the way home, he put-putted.

His wife seemed somewhat agitated and excited to see him, and exclaimed, "Darling, I have the most wonderful surprise for dinner tonight." She then blindfolded him and led him to his chair at the head of the dining room table. He seated himself, and just as she was ready to remove the blindfold, the telephone rang. She made him vow not to touch the blindfold until she returned, and then she went to answer the phone.

Seeing the opportunity, he shifted his weight to one leg and let go. It was not only loud, but ripe as rotten eggs. He took his napkin from his lap and vigorously fanned the air about him. Things had just returned to normal when he felt another urge coming on him.

He shifted to the other leg and let go again. This was a true prize winner. While keeping his ear on the conversation in the hall, he heard the phone farewells indicate the end of his freedom. He placed the napkin on his lap and folded his hands on top of it.

Smiling contentedly to himself, he was the very picture of innocence when his wife returned and was apologizing for taking so long. She asked if he had peeked and he assured her that he had not.

At this point, she removed the blindfold and there was his surprise...twelve dinner guests seated around the table for a Happy Birthday Dinner for him!

Attractive Grief-Stricken Widow

The attractive, grief-stricken widow had been living in seclusion at the home of her deceased husband's younger brother for several weeks. One evening, when she could no longer control her emotions, she barged into her brother-in-law's study and pleaded, "James, I want you to take off my dress."

The brother-in-law did as she requested. "Now," she continued, "take off my slip." He again complied. "And now," she said with a slight blush, "remove my panties and bra." Once more James obeyed her command.

Then, regaining her composure, she stared directly at the embarrassed young man and boldly announced, "I have only one more request, James. Don't ever let me catch you wearing my things again!"

Druggist Sisters

After rushing into a drugstore, the nervous young man was obviously embarrassed when a prim, middle-age woman asked if she could help him.

"N-no," he stammered, "I'd rather see the druggist."

"I'm the druggist," she responded cheerfully. "What can I do for you?"

"Oh...well, uh, it's nothing important," he said and turned to leave.

"Young man," said the woman, "my sister and I have been running this drugstore for nearly thirty years. There is nothing you can tell us that will embarrass us."

"Well, all right," he said. "I have this awful sexual hunger that nothing will appease. No matter how many times I make love, I still want to make love again. Is there anything you can give me for it?"

"Just a moment," said the little lady. "I'll have to discuss this with my sister."

A few minutes later she returned. "The best we can offer," she said, "is two hundred dollars a week and a half-interest in the business!"

Third String Quarterback

Two football teams are tied up 14-14. Fifty seconds are left in the game. The first-string quarterback is out with an injured leg. The second-string quarterback is out with a dislocated shoulder. They are down to the third-string quarterback, and folks, he's the worst quarterback that anybody's ever seen. Every time he hands the ball off, he fumbles. Every time he throws a pass, it's intercepted. But he's the team kicker and he can kick the dickens out of a football.

So, the coach gets him over there and says, "Alright, son, get in there. All I want you to do is run three quarterback sneaks and kick that ball just as far as you can kick it. Don't hand it off and don't pass it! Three quarterback sneaks and kick that ball as far as you can kick it. You got it?"

The kid says, "But coach..." The coach said, "Don't say a word, just get in there, three sneaks and punt!" So, in he goes. He takes the first snap on his own 15-yard line; a hole opens over right guard and he goes from his own 15-yard line to the 40 line. First down. Now the place is beginning to scream. Thirty five seconds left. He takes the second snap, another big hole opens, and he goes from his own 40-yard line to the other team's 25-yard line. Another first down. Now the place is going wild! Twenty five seconds left. He takes the third snap, goes from their 25-yard line all the way to the 1-yard line. First and goal! Ten seconds left...(punt sound). You guessed it, he kicked the ball out of the stadium!

The coach got him out to the sideline and said, "What on earth, WHAT ON EARTH, were you thinking when you kicked that ball?" And the kid said, "I was thinking about what a stupid coach we got."

Moral of the story: We must communicate! Sometimes less emphatically. Sometimes giving additional information.

Not Appreciated on Birthday

A friend of mine had a birthday recently. He got up and went down to breakfast, and his wife never wished him a happy birthday—never even mentioned that it was his birthday. He hugged all his children as he left for work, and none of them mentioned that it was his birthday. He was feeling pretty low.

When he got to work his secretary said, "Happy Birthday, Boss. Why don't we have lunch together today to celebrate your birthday. After lunch, we can have dessert at my place." After lunch, they arrive at her place and he is feeling really good about her remembering his birthday.

She leans over to him and whispers, "Excuse me for a minute while I change into something comfortable."

He said, "In a few minutes, her bedroom door opens and out came my secretary, my wife, and my kids carrying a birthday cake and singing Happy Birthday. There I stood with nothing on but my socks!"

Official Rules for Bedroom Golf

1. Each player will furnish his own equipment for play, normally one club and two balls.
2. Course to be played must be approved by the owner of the hole.
3. Unlike outdoor golf, the object is to get the club in the hole and keep the balls out of the hole.
4. For the most effective play, the club should have a firm shaft. Course owners are permitted to check the stiffness of the shaft before play begins.
5. Course owners reserve the right to restrict the length of the club to avoid damage to the hole.
6. The object of the game is to take as many strokes as necessary until course owner is satisfied. Failure to do so may result in being denied permission to play the course again.
7. It is usually considered bad form to begin playing the hole immediately upon arriving at the course. The experienced player will normally admire the entire course with special attention paid to well-formed bunkers.
8. Players are cautioned not to mention any other courses that they have played, or are currently playing, to the owner of the course being played. Upset owners have been known to damage the player's equipment for this reason.
9. Players should assure themselves that their match has been properly scheduled, especially on a different course being played for the first time. Previous players have been known to get irate if they find someone else playing what they considered to be their own private course.
10. Players should not assume a course is in shape for play at all times. Some owners may be embarrassed if their course is temporarily under

repair and the player is advised to use tact in this determination. More advanced players will find alternate means of play when this is the case.

11. It is considered an outstanding performance, time permitting, to play the same hole several times in one match.
12. Responsible bedroom golfers always use a golf bag.
13. Course owners shall be the sole judge of who the best player is.
14. Players are not permitted to tee off on the back nine without the express permission of the course owner!

Mysteries of the Night

The company commander and his first sergeant were in the field and had gone to bed for the night.

After some time, the sergeant woke up the officer and said, "Look up and tell me what you see."

The officer replied, "I see millions of stars."

"And what does that tell you?" asked the sergeant.

"Astronomically, it tells me that there are millions of galaxies and potentially billions of planets. Theologically, it tells me that God is great and we are small. Meteorologically, it tells me that tomorrow will be beautiful. What does it tell you, sergeant?"

"It tells me that somebody has stolen our tent," came the reply.

First Sermon

A new priest was so nervous about giving his first sermon at mass that he went to the monsignor and asked how he had handled nervousness.

The monsignor replied, "When I am worried about getting nervous on the pulpit, I put a glass of vodka next to the water glass. If I start to get nervous, I take a sip."

So next Sunday, he took the monsignor's advice. At the beginning of the sermon, he got nervous and took a drink. He proceeded to talk up a storm. Upon his return to the office after mass, he found the following note addressed to him on the door.

1. Sip the vodka, don't gulp.
2. There are 10 commandments, not 12.
3. There are 12 disciples, not 10.
4. Jesus was consecrated, not constipated.
5. Jacob wagered his donkey, he did not bet his ass.
6. We do not refer to Jesus Christ as the late J.C.
7. The Father, Son, and Holy Ghost are not referred to as Daddy, Junior and the Spook.
8. David slew Goliath, he did not kick the shit out of him.
9. When David was hit by a rock and was knocked off his donkey, don't say he was stoned off his ass.
10. We do not refer to the cross as the "Big T."
11. The Virgin Mary is not called "Mary with the Cherry."
12. When Jesus broke bread at the Last Supper he said, "Take this and eat it, for it is my body." He did not say, "Eat me."
13. The recommended grace before a meal is not, "Rub-A-Dub-Dub thanks for the grub, yeah God."
14. Next Sunday there will be a taffy pulling contest at St. Peter's, not a peter pulling contest at St Taffy's."

Halloween Party Costume

A lady and her husband are invited to a Halloween party and plan to attend. She goes out and gets a costume for each of them. That night, she gets a headache and doesn't feel like going. She insists that her husband go without her. He does and she falls back asleep. Later, she wakes up, her headache is gone, and she decides to go to the party. When she gets there, she sees her husband dancing with this woman and taking a few liberties with his hands. Since he hasn't seen her costume, she decides to dance with him to test him.

One thing leads to another, and she suggests that they go outside to his car and have some fun. The only requirement is that she not remove her costume head cover. After they go back inside, she slips away while he is dancing with someone else to go back home.

When her husband gets home, she says, "How was the dance darling?"

He said, "Oh, when I got there three other guys were there stag too, so we left and played poker. But I understand that the guy that I loaned my costume to had a great time!"

Assembly Line to Vice-President

During the noontime recreational activities, the president of the corporation mounted the platform, accompanied by an overall-clad man off the assembly line, and made this speech.

"Ladies and gentlemen, you are about to see how American industry rewards those who are conscientious and hard-working. This man standing beside me has been with the company less than a year. During this time, his unusual qualities have earned him salary increases in excess of one hundred dollars a week. I have watched him closely and observed with great pleasure the manner in which he has pitched in and gotten things done.

"Therefore, I am pleased to announce that starting this very afternoon he gets out of his work clothes, comes into the executive branch, and takes over an office with the title of Executive Vice President in Charge of Policy at an annual wage of eighty thousand dollars. Congratulations to you, sir."

The workman shook the extended hand and said, "Gee, thanks, Dad!"

Nonconforming Sparrow

Once upon a time, there was a nonconforming sparrow who decided not to fly south for the winter. However, soon the weather turned so cold that he reluctantly started to fly south. In a short time, ice began to form on his wings and he fell to earth in a barnyard, almost frozen.

A cow passed by and crapped on the little sparrow. The sparrow thought it was the end. But the manure warmed him and defrosted his wings.

Warm, happy, and able to breathe, the little sparrow started to sing. Just then a large cat came by, and hearing the chirping bird, it investigated the sound.

The cat cleared away the manure, found the chirping bird, and promptly ate him.

The Moral of the Story:

1. People who shit on you are not necessarily your enemies.
2. People who get you out of the shit are not necessarily your friends.
3. And finally, if you're warm and happy in a pile of shit, keep your mouth shut!

Circle Flies

A farmer got pulled over by a state trooper for speeding. The trooper started to lecture the farmer about his speed and to, in general, throw his weight around to try to make the farmer uncomfortable.

Finally, the trooper got around to writing out the ticket. As he began writing, he kept swatting at some flies that were buzzing around his head.

The farmer said, “Having some problems with circle flies there, are ya?”

The trooper stopped writing the ticket and said, “Well, yeah if that’s what they are. I never heard of circle flies.”

So the farmer said, “Well, circle flies are common on farms. See, they’re called circle flies because they are most always found circling around the back end of a horse.”

The trooper said, “Oh.” And went back to writing the ticket.

Then, after a minute, he stopped and said, “Hey...wait a minute, are you trying to call me a horse’s ass?”

The farmer said, “Oh, no, officer. I have too much respect for law enforcement and police officers to even think about calling you a horse’s ass.”

The trooper said, “Well, that’s a good thing,” and went back to writing the ticket.

After a long pause, the farmer said, “Hard to fool them flies though.”

Captain at Sea

One night at sea, the ship's captain saw what looked like the lights of another ship heading toward him. He had his signalman blink to the other ship: "Change your course 10 degrees south."

The reply came back: "Change your course 10 degrees north."

The ship's captain answered: "I am a captain, change your course south."

The reply was: "Well, I am a seaman first class. Change your course north."

This infuriated the captain, so he signaled back: "Dammit, I say change your course south. I'm on a battleship!"

The reply came back: "And I say change your course north. I'm in a lighthouse."

Moral: You must make sure that you have all the correct information before making a decision.

Church Communications

1. The sermon this morning: "Jesus Walks on the Water." The sermon tonight: "Searching for Jesus."
2. Our youth basketball team is back in action Wednesday at 8 p.m. in the recreation hall. Come out and watch us kill Christ the King.
3. Announcement in the church bulletin for a national Fasting and Prayer Conference: The cost of attending the Fasting and Prayer Conference includes meals.
4. "Ladies, don't forget the rummage sale. It's a chance to get rid of those things not worth keeping around the house. Don't forget your husbands."
5. The peacemaking meeting scheduled for today has been cancelled due to a conflict!
6. Don't let worry kill you off—let the church help.
7. For those of you who have children and don't know it, we have a nursery downstairs.
8. Next Thursday there will be tryouts for the choir. They need all the help they can get.
9. Eight new choir robes are currently needed due to the addition of several new members and to the deterioration of some older ones.
10. Scouts are saving aluminum cans, bottles, and other items to be recycled. Proceeds will be used to cripple children.
11. Please place your donation in the envelope along with the deceased person you want remembered.
12. Attend and you will hear an excellent speaker and heave a healthy lunch.
13. Ladies' Bible Study will be held Thursday morning at 10 a.m. All ladies are invited to lunch in the Fellowship Hall after the BS is done.
14. Our next song is: "Angels We Have Heard Get High."

15 Weight Watchers will meet at 7 p.m. at the First Presbyterian Church. Please use the large double door at the side entrance.
16. The Associate Minister unveiled the church's new tithing campaign slogan last Sunday: "I Upped My Pledge—Up Yours."
17. Low Self Esteem Support Group will meet Thursday at 7 p.m. Please use the back door.
18. The eighth-graders will be presenting Shakespeare's Hamlet in the church basement on Friday at 7 p.m. The congregation is invited to attend this tragedy.
19. The ladies of the church have cast off clothing of every kind. They may be seen in the basement on Friday afternoon.

Husband's Marriage Counselor

The husband was disturbed by his wife's indifferent attitude towards him and the marriage counselor suggested he try being more aggressive in his lovemaking.

"Act more like a romantic lover and less like a bored spouse," he was advised. "When you go home, make love to her as soon as you meet, even if it is right inside the front door."

At the next consultation, the adviser was pleased to hear that the husband had followed his instructions. "And how did she react this time?" the consultant asked.

"Well, to tell you the truth," the husband replied, "she was still sort of indifferent. But one thing I've got to admit, her bridge club went absolutely wild!"

Like the Way You Think

A teacher asks her class, "If there are 5 birds sitting on a fence and you shoot one of them, how many will be left?"

She calls on little Johnny. He replies, "None, they will all fly away with the first gun shot."

The teacher replies, "The correct answer is 4, but I like your thinking."

Then, little Johnny says, "I have a question for you.

"There are three women sitting on a bench having ice cream. One is delicately licking the sides of the triple scoop of ice cream. The second is gobbling down the top and sucking the cone. The third is biting off the top of the ice cream. Which one is married?"

The teacher, blushing a great deal, replied, "Well I suppose the one that's gobbled down the top and sucked the cone."

To which Johnny replied, "The correct answer is the one with the wedding ring on...but I like your thinking."

Pop Quiz

"A professor gives his physiology class a pop quiz. One question he asks is "What part of the human anatomy expands to ten times its normal size during periods of intense emotion and excitement?"

He picks a rather overdressed girl in the front row to answer it. "Miss Callahan!"

The indicated girl, who heard the question, stammers with some embarrassment: "Professor, I'd rather not answer that question."

The professor says, "That's all right, Miss Callahan, you don't need to answer it. Is there anyone present that can answer it?" He notes an interested face in the back of the classroom. "Mr. Hawkins!"

Hawkins says, "Yes, Professor, it is the pupil of the eye that expands to ten times its normal size during periods of emotion and excitement."

The professor says, "That is correct, Mr. Hawkins." Then he turns to Miss Callahan. He says, "Young lady, two things are obvious from your reaction to the question. One, you haven't studied this week's assignment and Two, I'm afraid marriage is going to be a tremendous disappointment to you."

As the rabbit said when he sat on a cake of ice:

“My tale is told.”

I sincerely hope that reading this book has brought you more than a few smiles and laughs.

EAA

About the Author

Born and raised in Central Florida, Art grew up in the small town of Lake Wales, Florida. His dad owned several orange groves, and he and his two brothers helped work in the groves from an early age. His sister helped his mom with the cooking and housework—which was a lot with the dirt constantly tracked in from the groves.

After Art completed high school, he enrolled as one of the charter students at the opening of the University of South Florida in Tampa, Florida. After two years, he was called into active duty with the U.S. Navy. Having been in the Navy Reserves, he had already reached the level of Petty Officer Third Class, Personnelman. During his time on active duty, he made two trips to the Mediterranean Sea and married a local girl from Winter Haven, Florida. From this marriage, Art's daughter, Christi Albritton Bass, was born. After sixteen years, that marriage ended with Art having full custody of his eight-year-old daughter.

Sometime later Art met the love of his life, Anita Day Albritton, and they were married approximately three years later. When they first met, Nita was 19, and Art was 38 with an eight-year-old daughter. Nita and Christi worked out wonderfully, but Nita desperately wanted children of her own. After seven years, (without the help of a government man-see jokes) with the help of in vitro fertilization, the final attempt was successful and Nita was pregnant—with twins! Alex and Andrew were born, and as reflected in the anecdotes to come, brought great joy into the family.

During all of this, Art was employed by State Farm Insurance Companies at their regional office in Winter Haven. After 38 years, he retired to have more time with Nita and his now 10-year-old boys, Christi and her husband Dave, and their two children, Daniel and Eliana (Art's grandkids).

The anecdotes are from all of his interesting experiences, and his favorite jokes were collected during these times. His love of life is reflected well by both.

Made in the USA
Columbia, SC
03 May 2024

34715702R00102